100 THINGS BEARS FANS SHOULD KNOW & DO BEFORE THEY DIE

100 THINGS BEARS FANS SHOULD KNOW & DO BEFORE THEY DIE

Kent McDill

Library of Congress Cataloging-in-Publication Data available upon request.

This book is available in quantity at special discounts for your group or organization. For further information, contact:

Triumph Books LLC
814 North Franklin Street
Chicago, Illinois 60610
(312) 337-0747
www.triumphbooks.com

Printed in U.S.A.
ISBN: 978-1-62937-836-7
Design by Patricia Frey
Photos courtesy of AP Images unless otherwise indicated

This book is dedicated to the memory of my father, K.B. McDill, who was a huge Bears fan, and to my mother, Marilyn, who was always my biggest fan.

Contents

Foreword

Nothing stirs the passions of some 4.6 million Chicagoans more than the Bears. It's a generational bond handed down from one decade to the next. Sixteen individual dramas promoted with frenzied analysis; trumpeted by wins, ruined by losses. It's the "game" and *everything* it means—from personal and civic pride to bragging rights—that is uniquely crafted to yank the emotion from an adoring fan base. I see it, I hear it, and I feel it every NFL Sunday.

In Chicago, that fan base is uniquely loyal. Soldier Field is on a 28-year sellout streak, with more than 21,000 fans on a season-ticket waiting list. Surveys from Scarborough Sports Marketing found that 63 percent of Chicago area residents "identify themselves as Bears fans." In the 2012–13 season, the average Bears television rating dominated at 29.2. The radio listening audience for Bears games is the largest in the NFL, 56 percent higher than the next closest team.

There is a symbiotic relationship between the franchise and the hardworking, blue-collar city. It has been captured over the last five years by Chicago-based marketing agency Two by Four. In black and white terms, their creative campaigns define the important connection between the team and its fans.

The agency debuted in 2008 its "One City, One Team" campaign focusing on the passion of the casual to the hardcore Bears fan. The inspiration came from a quote by team owner Virginia McCaskey, the daughter of George Halas: "Baseball divides Chicago; football unites." Actual fans, not models, were used in billboard ads and television spots. One of the billboards said it all: "If you're not a fan, you're a tourist."

This is a nine-time championship franchise, but only two have been won since 1946. That's a lot of disappointment over the last

67 years, but the importance of the shared values reflected in the fans, the Bears, and the city supersedes wins and losses. Football is a metaphor for life in the big city. You get knocked down, you get back up.

For me, nothing tops an autumn Sunday in Chicago: Lake Shore Drive early in the morning. The smell of charcoal before breakfast. The silent intensity of walking into an empty stadium, being prepped for the main event. The anticipation of what is to come. The green grass. Navy blue and orange. The adrenaline rush that is NFL football.

Road trips are mini-retreats for a growing number of Bears fans, who flock to the team hotel by the hundreds to greet the Bears in virtually every NFL city, with the exception of Green Bay. More often than not, the road stadiums are beginning to feel like home games if the scoreboard says so. And the fans are not easily dismissed. They stay. They scream. They chant. They party. They love their team.

About 90 minutes before kickoff of Super Bowl XLI in Miami, Florida, in 2006, I walked through Sun Life Stadium and up into the nosebleed section. There was palpable optimism in the air. Bears fans decorated the seats in their own style and substance. These were not gifted donations from corporate types, many were the homegrown, generational fans who live and die with every snap, whistle, and tackle.

They were kind enough to share their stories; mostly how long they've been Bears fans, how long they've owned season tickets, detailing their expectations for the game, and taking pictures of the rare moments shared with friends and family. I found one woman literally in tears overjoyed by her opportunity to be in the building, anxiously and nervously awaiting the opening kickoff.

And what an opening kickoff it was.

Rookie Devin Hester's touchdown in his own backyard of Miami, never done before or since in Super Bowl history, was as memorable as it gets. It's those memories that stand the test of time. Forever shared and reviewed in a very personal way.

Each NFL season is a humbling journey for me and my broadcast partner (and eight-year Chicago Bear guard) Tom Thayer. We understand the magnitude of each game and what it means to the millions of Bears supporters here, there, and everywhere across the globe. Every thing matters. It's an obsession.

The 94th season of Bears football is around the corner, and I'll be "calling it like I'm loving it" for the most passionate fans in the NFL.

Can't wait.

—Jeff Joniak
May 2013

1 George Halas

George Halas and the Chicago Bears are synonymous. There could not be one without the other.

Halas created the Chicago Bears, coached them for 40 seasons in four different stints, and led them to eight NFL championships (six as coach). He pioneered the NFL's progress from its early stages. He engineered a profit-sharing plan as the extremely successful Bears propped up the other teams in the NFL when they struggled to make money.

Halas found Mike Ditka as a player and hired him as a coach. He helped create the rivalry between the Bears and the Green Bay Packers. He installed the T-formation that was used by football teams for decades. He found Dick Butkus and Gale Sayers. He named the team himself.

There would be no Chicago Bears without George Halas. He is the only person about whom that can be said.

Halas was born in Chicago before the turn of the 20th century. He died in Chicago in 1983. Thirty years later, the Bears uniform still included the football-shaped emblem bearing the initials GSH to represent the memory of George Stanley Halas.

Halas' football career started at the University of Illinois, where he was a member of the 1918 Big Ten champion Illini team. He scored a touchdown in the 1919 Rose Bowl, playing for the Great Lakes Naval Training Station team.

In 1920, he joined the A.E. Staley Company of Decatur, Illinois, as a sales representative. He also served as the player-coach for the company's football team, and was the team's representative at a meeting held in Canton, Ohio, which created the American Professional Football Association, the precursor to the NFL.

In 1921, the Staley Company turned the team over to Halas, who moved the club to Chicago, and he created a team good enough to win the 1921 APFA championship. At the time, the team was known as the Chicago Staleys.

The team became known as the Chicago Bears in 1922 (Halas eventually came to be known as "Papa Bear"). Halas played wide receiver and defensive end for the team for the remainder of the '20s, and coached it as well. He played and coached until 1929, when he kicked himself upstairs to serve as the team's owner. He became sole owner of the team in 1932. He returned to coach the team again in 1933, and coached the club for another 10 years while also serving as owner. Under Halas' leadership, the Bears won NFL titles in 1940 and 1941.

In 1936, in order to preserve some order in signing players, Halas spearheaded a new rule that would state the NFL (the league changed its name in 1922) would not sign players who had not graduated from college.

Halas signed up for a stint in the Navy in 1942 to serve during World War II. He handed control of the Bears over to former Bears player and Detroit Lions coach Heartley "Hunk" Anderson and former Bears player Luke Johnsos, who ran the club until 1946. Halas returned to the Bears after World War II in 1946 and coached the club for another decade, winning a title in his first year back. He did not coach the team in 1956 or 1957, but came back yet again to coach from 1958 to 1967, winning a championship in 1963. He retired from coaching in 1968 with a career record of 324 wins, 151 losses, and 31 ties.

After retiring from coaching, Halas remained the active owner of the Bears until his death in 1983.

With the help of University of Chicago coach Clark Shaughnessy, Halas created football's T-formation, a structured offensive plan that called for a great deal of movement and strong running out of the backfield. He lured University of Illinois star Red Grange to the Bears in 1925 at a time when the league was in need of prestige.

Halas built the 1963 NFL champion Bears, whose roster included the legendary likes of tight end Mike Ditka, defensive end Doug Atkins, fullback Rick Casares, linebacker Joe Fortunato, linebacker Bill George, flanker Johnny Morris, defensive end Ed O'Bradovich, safety Richie Petitbon, and quarterback Billy Wade. That team remained favored sons in Chicago for the next 20-plus years, until the Bears won Super Bowl XX after the 1985 season.

In 1982, just a year from his death, Halas made a significant move for the Bears, hiring former Bears tight end Mike Ditka to coach the team. Ditka had no head coaching experience but led the team to its only Super Bowl win in 1985, and that created a long-standing tradition of the Bears hiring first-time head coaches for the franchise.

The George S. Halas Trophy is still awarded to the winner of the NFL's National Football Conference, of which the Bears are a member. He was voted into the Pro Football Hall of Fame in 1963.

In 2019, in celebration of the NFL's 100th year of existence, Halas was selected as one of the 10 best coaches in the league's history.

2 Walter Payton

The 1970s did not start out well for the Chicago Bears. In fact, since the fabled 1963 championship season, the Bears had only two winning seasons until 1977.

In 1972, star running back Gale Sayers was forced to retire after just seven seasons in the NFL due to injury. The next year, famed linebacker Dick Butkus, the pride of the University of Illinois, also had to leave the game due to injuries. Two legends were gone, each without a championship, and the team was floundering in mediocrity.

George Halas was fed up with the fortunes of his team, and in 1974 he made a momentous decision, hiring Jim Finks away from the Minnesota Vikings to be the team's first general manager to handle most of the daily football operations. Prior to that, Halas had run the show almost by himself, especially in the area of player acquisitions.

In 1975, Finks selected Walter Payton, a running back out of Jackson State University in Mississippi, with the fourth pick in the NFL draft. Things began to turn around from that point.

Payton played 13 seasons for the Bears. By the time he was done playing, he owned the NFL's record for most career rushing yards and touchdowns. He was also the all-time leader in rushing carries, a record he was most proud of.

But Payton's accomplishments on the field were only part of his legacy with the Bears. His unflagging enthusiasm for the game, and the power and strength with which he played, made him a favorite of the Chicago crowd. Add to that a lively personality that led him to be called "Sweetness" and you had one of the most popular football players in Chicago history.

Walter Payton runs over Lem Barney for a touchdown in a game against the Detroit Lions in his rookie season, 1975.

Payton was one of the few players who ever smiled consistently on the field. You could just tell he was having a good time.

Payton was an accomplished college player, and upon completing his career at Jackson State he owned the NCAA's record for scoring with 65 rushing touchdowns. But his first NFL season was not much of a success, scoring just seven touchdowns and gaining less than 700 yards in 14 games.

But by his second year in the pros, Payton had it figured out. He scored 13 touchdowns in 1976, made his first Pro Bowl, and he used that as a springboard for the next season, when he rushed for 1,852 yards and scored 16 touchdowns. Starting in 1976, Payton had more than 1,000 yards rushing for each of the next 10 seasons, not counting the strike-shortened 1982 season.

By 1977, the league knew what Payton was all about. His running style was powerful, and his moves were slick. But his best "talent" as a football player was his willingness to make contact with defenders. Payton became famous for his stiff arm, held out in front of him to force away would-be tacklers. He was also well-known for his desire to gain extra yards with effort after being hit, or almost brought down.

Payton even showed his desire to advance the ball once he was on the ground. He developed a signature move of reaching his hand out with the ball, extending his arm as far as possible to place the ball down a yard beyond where he had touched down, hoping the referees would make a mistake in placing the ball and give the Bears yet another few inches.

Payton also made himself known for what he did when he wasn't carrying the football. He was a tremendous blocking back for those times when the fullback was assigned to carry the ball, or the quarterback was trying a bootleg.

The Bears did not need to hand the ball off to Payton to get him to have an effect on the game. He excelled as a receiver, with 492 career receptions and 15 touchdown catches in his career. The play-action worked well when the fake handoff was to Payton, who then ended up with the ball in his hands anyway.

Payton also served as the Bears' emergency punter, and its third-string quarterback. Payton still holds the record for most touchdown passes thrown by a non-quarterback, with eight.

From 1975 to 1983, Payton got to play in two playoff games, losing them both. But Payton's opportunity to win an NFL title grew with the hiring of former Bears tight end Mike Ditka as coach in 1982. Ditka, the hard-nosed, no-nonsense, argumentative player from an earlier era of football, saw a kindred spirit in Payton. They both would go to the greatest lengths to succeed on the football field.

And under Ditka, Payton did succeed. He gained 1,421 yards and had six touchdowns in 1983, his first full season under Ditka (the 1982 season was a strike-shortened campaign), then gained 1,684 yards the next season as the Bears improved to 10–6. In the 1985 season, the Bears went 15–1, cruised through the NFC playoffs to make the Super Bowl for the first time, then crushed the New England Patriots 46–10, one of the most lopsided Super Bowls in history. That season Payton averaged 4.8 yards per carry, the most since his best statistical season of 1977 when he averaged 5.5 yards per carry.

Although Payton scored 11 touchdowns and gained 1,551 yards rushing on the way to the Super Bowl, and although the Bears scored four offensive touchdowns in the title game, Payton did not score in the championship game. That fact is considered the saddest, most regrettable aspect of his playing career.

Payton played through the 1987 season. At the end of his career, he owned the NFL records for most rushing yards, most rushing touchdowns, most rushing attempts, most yards from scrimmage, and most all-purpose yards. He was inducted into the Pro Football Hall of Fame in 1993.

In 1999, Payton was diagnosed with primary sclerosing cholangitis, a rare liver disease, and died in November of 1999 at the young age of 45 from cholangiocarcinoma.

In 1999, the NFL changed the name of its Man of the Year Award to the Walter Payton NFL Man of the Year Award, given to a player noted for excellence on the field combined with his volunteer and charity work.

Twelve running backs were selected as members of the NFL's top 100 players in history as part of the league's celebration of its 100th year of existence, and Payton was one of those 12.

3 The 1985 Super Bowl

The city of Chicago was incorporated in 1837. The Chicago Cubs and White Sox began playing baseball at the end of the 19th century, and through 2013 appeared in 17 World Series or baseball championships combined. The Chicago Bulls won six NBA championships in the 1990s, and provided the stage for Michael Jordan to become the city's favorite athlete of all time, and perhaps the most famous athlete in any sport ever.

But no sporting event captured the city, or remained close to the hearts of the populous, the way the 1985 Chicago Bears did following their majestic victory in Super Bowl XX.

The first Super Bowl ever was not called the Super Bowl. It was called the First World Championship Game, marking the first time the AFL and NFL champions played against each other after the old AFL merged with the NFL. It was a game between the Green Bay Packers and the Kansas City Chiefs, played in January of 1967 following the 1966 season. Today it is referred to as Super Bowl I.

Although the Chicago Bears won eight professional football championships prior to the invention of the Super Bowl, they did not reach the ultimate game of the modern NFL until the 1985 season, when they marched through the regular season 15–1, shut out the New York Giants and Los Angeles Rams in the playoffs to make it to the game, and then embarrassed the AFC champion New England Patriots on the way to a 46–10 Super Bowl victory.

The city of Chicago changed that day (January 26, 1986, to be exact). A season-long love affair with the 1985 Chicago Bears became a never-ending fairy tale romance. The 1985 Bears, who had the most dominant defense in the history of the

NFL, the most popular player in Chicago Bears history (Walter Payton), the most unusual player in NFL history (William "the Refrigerator" Perry), and the coach who would eventually turn into a pop culture caricature (Mike Ditka), became the greatest team in Chicago history.

Following a 15–1 regular season (the only loss coming on a Monday night in Miami against the Dolphins), the Bears shut out the New York Giants 21–0 in the division playoff game. In the NFC Championship Game, the Bears again pulled off a shutout, blanking the Los Angeles Rams 24–0 on a cold day at Soldier Field.

The Bears got to the Super Bowl as the most colorful and polarizing team in recent NFL history. They released a video titled "The Super Bowl Shuffle," which built upon their reputation as a team that played hard and celebrated well. That the Bears filmed the video prior to heading to New Orleans to play in the Super Bowl showed just how supremely confident they were. The fact they backed up the video with a resounding victory only nailed down their stature among Bears and NFL fans.

Super Bowl XX was played in New Orleans, a perfect place for a team of characters like the Bears to strut their stuff. Led by the charismatic and bombastic coach Mike Ditka, the Bears made the buildup to the game unlike any other. Their pregame press conferences filled reporters' notebooks all week, and reports of the players out partying at night were rampant. If any team ever entered the Super Bowl with the appearance of an overconfident bunch ready for an upset, it was the Bears.

But the Bears were as good as advertised, and as dominant defensively as any team in league history. The New England Patriots, the AFC champions, had an 11–5 regular season record and had to win three road playoff games to get into the Super Bowl. The Patriots had no chance in the championship game, which the Bears won 46–10, the largest margin of victory for a Super Bowl up to that point. It was also the most points scored by the winning team in a Super Bowl.

Amazingly, the Patriots actually held a lead in the game, scoring 79 seconds into the contest on a field goal set up by a fumble by Walter Payton. The Bears tied the game at the 5:40 mark of the first quarter on a field goal by Kevin Butler, who gave the Bears the lead for good on a field goal at the 13:34 mark of the first quarter to make it 6–3. The Bears scored again just before the end of the quarter on an 11-yard run by fullback Matt Suhey and had a 13–3 lead going into the second quarter.

The Bears scored 10 more points in the second quarter on a touchdown run by quarterback Jim McMahon and a third field goal by Butler as time expired. The halftime score was 23–3. But the Bears were just getting warmed up.

They scored 21 points in just four minutes in the third quarter: on a touchdown run by McMahon (who became the first quarterback to rush for two touchdowns in the Super Bowl); an interception return for a score by Reggie Phillips; and one of the most famous touchdowns in Super Bowl history, the one-yard plunge by William "the Refrigerator" Perry, the 335-pound defensive lineman turned into a fullback by Ditka.

The Bears allowed a touchdown pass in the fourth quarter—the only TD scored against them in the playoffs—and got a late safety to finish the scoring.

Having won the Super Bowl by 36 points, the Bears still had reason to bemoan the results because star running back Walter Payton, who at that point had toiled 11 seasons for the Bears without a championship, failed to score in the game. The touchdown run by Perry was often criticized as the best chance Payton had to score, and it was taken by a player used as both an unusual offensive weapon and as a publicity stunt. Over the years, several players said the Patriots had targeted Payton defensively the entire game, making sure he did not score on them.

The stout Bears defense held the Patriots to 123 yards in total offense, while the Bears offense was credited with 408 yards. The time of possession in the game displayed the Bears' dominance, as the Bears held the ball for 39:15 of the game while the Patriots had the ball for just 20:45.

The thinking was that a member of the Bears' defense had to win the Most Valuable Player Award, so it was given to defensive end Richard Dent, who had 1.5 sacks in the game. He became only the fourth defensive player in 20 years to win the Super Bowl MVP Award.

Mike Ditka became the second man in the Super Bowl era to win the Super Bowl first as a player (in 1972 with the Dallas Cowboys) and then as head coach.

4 Mike Ditka (the Coach)

After retiring from playing in 1972 after four seasons with the Dallas Cowboys, Ditka was immediately hired by the Cowboys to serve as an assistant coach working with the tight ends, and he stayed with the Cowboys for nine seasons. He got another championship ring with the Cowboys when they won the Super Bowl following the 1977 season.

But in some ways Ditka's heart remained with the Bears, who had drafted him in 1961 and set him apart from all other tight ends by making him a significant offensive weapon rather than just an extra blocking option on the offensive line. Even while working with Dallas, Ditka suffered over the way his relationship ended with Bears owner George Halas in 1966, when Halas traded him to Philadelphia after an argument over salary.

Mike Ditka and Jim McMahon share a few words during the Bears' January 5, 1986, playoff victory over the New York Giants.

So while still with the Cowboys, Ditka wrote a letter to Halas asking him to consider hiring Ditka as head coach when he deemed Ditka ready to take over a team.

In 1982, after firing coach Neill Armstrong following a 6–10 season, Halas recalled the letter and took a chance by rehiring his former player as the new coach of the Bears.

In the book *'63: the Story of the 1963 World Champion Chicago Bears,* Ditka recalled his initial conversation with Halas.

"That 1963 team was the best football team without question that George Halas ever coached," Ditka said, referring to the team Ditka played with that won the NFL title. "When George Halas hired me in 1982, he had one request. 'I want you to bring this thing back to what it was in '63.' I told him I didn't know if we can get those kind of players, but if we can, we will have the same attitude and zeal that those guys had. I promised him that."

With Halas' obvious blessing, Ditka took over and immediately placed his stamp on the team. Coaching at the age of 43, Ditka proved to be the fiery kind of coach that Halas was, and he got results in quick fashion. Bears players already knew Ditka from his sideline performances as the Cowboys assistant coach, throwing clipboards and stomping around, red-faced with anger.

But upon accepting the coaching job, Ditka held a team meeting in which he promised the players a Super Bowl title if they would stick with him and play the game the way he wanted it played.

Ditka's personality was colorful, sometimes too much so. He often argued with fans, including Bears fans, and was famous for the things he would yell at the Soldier Field faithful after losses. His postgame press conferences after losses were not to be missed, either, as he argued with reporters or sometimes ignored them entirely.

The Bears were 3–6 in Ditka's first season, 1982, which was shortened by a player's strike. The Bears went 8–8 in 1983, and in 1984 the Bears won the Central Division but lost to San Francisco in the NFC Championship Game.

In 1985, the Bears went 15–1 and cruised through the playoffs and the Super Bowl to claim the team's first championship since that 1963 team.

That Super Bowl, as spectacular as it was, included two climatic events that will never be forgotten. Ditka, who was in charge of the offense for the team, was unable to get a touchdown for legendary running back Walter Payton, despite the fact the Bears scored 46 points in the game. Quarterback Jim McMahon ran in for two touchdowns, Perry scored the Bears' last touchdown of the game, and Payton went scoreless.

Also, the Super Bowl saw the ignominy of defensive coordinator Buddy Ryan getting carried off the field by his players as Ditka was carried off by the offense. That show of support for Ryan, with whom Ditka had feuded almost since their association began, left a bad taste in Ditka's mouth as he found himself sharing credit for the success of one of the best teams in NFL history. Ryan, who had been with the team since before Ditka was hired, left the Bears after the 1985 season to become head coach of the Philadelphia Eagles.

The 1985 Super Bowl made superstars out of many of the Bears, and Ditka led the parade. He became an oft-seen product endorser, taking advantage of his newfound stardom while urging his players to stay focused on football.

Halas, Ditka's mentor of sorts, died in 1983 and didn't get to see the team win under Ditka. But Halas' death also changed the nature of the front office of the Bears, as Halas' grandson, Michael McCaskey, took over the reins. Ditka and McCaskey had an adversarial relationship often related to player acquisition, and Ditka was eventually fired by McCaskey after the 1992 season.

As coach of the Bears, Ditka had a record of 106–62 and led the team to the NFC Championship Game three times in 11 years, including the Super Bowl year.

Several years later, Ditka and the New Orleans Saints both seemed to make a mistake when the Saints hired Ditka to coach the team. In three years, the Saints went 15–33 under Ditka, and he ended his coaching career after the 1999 season.

Since Ditka practically invented the tight end position as it is played today, it makes sense that he was one of five tight ends added to the NFL's list of top 100 players in 2019 to celebrate the league's 100 years of existence.

5 Soldier Field

At the turn of the 20th century, the city of Chicago was still trying to prove its worth and earn a mark among the world's elite cities. The Chicago lakefront had been recreated with landfill to hold a new and massive municipal park, but the city wanted to have new structures that could someday host a major international event such as an Olympics or World's Fair.

Because it was Chicago, politics got involved, but eventually, all of the machinations were complete and the city got its first expo-type outdoor stadium on the lakefront. Initially named Grant Park Stadium, the facility was opened in the fall of 1924 but had its name changed to Soldier Field one year later to honor the soldiers who had fought in the recently ended First World War. Soldier Field is now and always was owned and operated by the Chicago Park District.

The first event held at Soldier Field was an athletic competition among the city's policemen in honor of the Chicago Police Benevolent Association in September of 1924.

When Soldier Field opened, it held seating for more than 74,000 fans, but it did not become the home of the city's NFL franchise until 1971, when the team moved from Wrigley Field on the city's north side. But Soldier Field was famous for its football games played there long before the Bears signed up and moved in.

The first football game played at Soldier Field was on October 4, 1924, between Chicago's Austin High School and Louisville's Male High School. In 1926, before a crowd of 100,000 in the stadium's temporary reconfiguration, Army and Navy played for the national championship. In 1927, the stadium was again

College All-Star Football Game

Arch Ward, the longtime sports editor of the *Chicago Tribune*, invented an exhibition football game to be played between a team of football players recently graduated from college against the most recent champion of the NFL. The game started in 1934, and was always played in Chicago's Soldier Field, except for two years during World War II, when it was moved to Dyche Stadium on the campus of Northwestern University.

The game was played every year through 1976 with the exception of 1974 (because of a player's strike), and the NFL champion played every year except 1935, when the runner-up Bears played in the game rather than the champion New York Giants.

The Bears played in the game seven times. They won five times, lost once, and tied once.

In the 42 games, the All-Stars won just nine times, and tied twice, including one time against the Bears.

reconfigured to hold 123,000 for a game between Notre Dame and the University of Southern California.

In 1926, the first professional football game was played at Soldier Field. The Chicago Bears and Chicago Cardinals, rivals in the NFL, played a charity game called the Armistice Day Game. Through the years, until the Cardinals moved to St. Louis in 1960, the Bears and Cardinals played numerous charity games at Soldier Field, although Wrigley Field remained the Bears' home field until 1971.

Before the Bears moved in, the stadium hosted numerous high school football games; national and international soccer matches; and the College All-Star Game, a summer contest sponsored by the *Chicago Tribune* that brought graduating college football players to play against the previous year's NFL champion. That game was played from 1934 to 1976.

Although the Bears made Soldier Field their permanent home field in 1971, they played games at the lakefront stadium for years. The Bears annually hosted the Armed Forces Game, a preseason exhibition, starting in 1945, occasionally playing the game at Soldier Field.

The Bears moved into Soldier Field in 1971 because they were forced out of Wrigley Field by the NFL, which wanted the team to have a larger stadium with permanent seating (Wrigley was configured with temporary seats for NFL games to build up attendance). Their first game in their now-permanent home stadium was September 19, 1971, against the Pittsburgh Steelers, won by the Bears 17–15.

At the time the Bears moved into Soldier Field, the stadium was being criticized in Chicago for being unsafe, dilapidated, and too small. Renovations were made at the time to increase seating and safety; Astroturf was installed to improve the playing field.

In 1988, the CPD returned the field to natural grass. Despite continued improvements in artificial grass surfaces and constant criticism about the playing surface in November and December games in Chicago, as of 2013 the CPD has never changed the surface back to an artificial grass field.

Soldier Field was almost never an ideal home for the Bears, and plans were suggested often for the Bears to build stadiums elsewhere so they could move into a more modern and larger facility. But none of the plans ever reached fruition.

In 2001, the Chicago Park District announced plans to renovate the interior of Soldier Field while leaving the historic exterior intact. Although the plan was met with wide, wild criticism, the CPD went ahead and forced the Bears out of Soldier Field. For the 2002 season, the Bears played their home games at the University of Illinois football field in Champaign, two hours south of Chicago.

While the renovation provided the Bears and the Park District with new revenue streams from luxury boxes and club seats, the new configuration made Soldier Field the smallest NFL stadium in terms of available seating (61,500).

In 2010, the NFL started contemplating allowing cold-weather cities to host the Super Bowl. Detroit hosted in 2006 at the domed Ford Field downtown, and when a new open-air stadium was built in East Rutherford, New Jersey, for the New York Jets and Giants, the 2014 Super Bowl was scheduled for that site. But Chicago was never given any consideration due to the small number of seats at Soldier Field.

6 Sid Luckman

Sid Luckman was the best Bears quarterback ever. Even as the NFL has moved toward more passing and offense and scoring, no one in a Bears uniform has come close to what Luckman accomplished.

Luckman, born of Jewish immigrants in Brooklyn, played for the Bears from 1939 to 1950. He led the Bears to four NFL championships. He was the field general for a new attack formation, the T-formation, which was designed by former Stanford coach Clark Shaughnessy and adopted by Bears owner and coach George Halas. The formation was run to endless efficiency by Luckman.

Luckman was a successful college tailback at Columbia University in a time when the tailback, not the quarterback, did most of the passing. But Halas needed a player to run his new system of offense, and upon watching Luckman play in a game in New York, recruited the reluctant player to quit working at his father-in-law's trucking company and move to Chicago to play for the Bears.

What happened next rarely occurs in sports. A single athlete combined with a new approach to create an offense that not only succeeded, but lasted decades. Luckman and the T-formation revolutionized football and brought the Bears newfound respect in the NFL.

Luckman's numbers were extraordinary for the time. He passed for 14,686 yards, had 137 touchdown passes, and only 132 interceptions in 128 games. He completed 51.8 percent of his passes. But it was his unusual intelligence that allowed him to run the complicated multifaceted offense that, prior to his arrival, was used by colleges but limited in the pro game.

The success started in 1940, Luckman's second season with the Bears. With the help of two years of great draft choices, including running back Bill Osmanski, center/linebacker Clyde Turner, guard Ray Bray, and end Ken Kavanaugh, the Bears won the 1940 NFL title with a revenge win over the Washington Redskins, 73–0, the largest margin of victory ever in the NFL. Earlier that season, the Redskins had beaten the Bears 7–3, creating a contentious relationship between the teams.

Luckman actually had a below-average season in 1940, completing less than 50 percent of his passes and throwing nine interceptions to just four touchdowns. But his numbers improved from there as he got accustomed to the T-formation. In 1943, he had a quarterback rating of 107.5 with 28 touchdown passes to 12 interceptions. He completed 110 passes on 202 attempts. Just in case you don't have a calculator handy, that means he threw a touchdown pass on almost 14 percent of his attempts, a statistic that has never been approached in the pros since.

Luckman still owns an NFL record. At the Polo Grounds in New York, on November 14, 1943, when he was being honored as a local boy made good, Luckman threw for seven touchdowns, which is still tied for the most touchdown passes in one game in the history of the NFL. He threw two passes to Jim Benton and Hampton Pool, and one each to Connie Mack Berry, Harry Clarke, and George Wilson. His numbers that day were 21 completions on 32 passes for 433 yards. His 28 touchdown passes that season (obviously, one-quarter of them in one game) were compiled over just 10 games, and that record stood for many years.

Luckman was named the NFL's Most Valuable Player in 1943 and retired in 1950 having won four titles.

7 Packers-Bears Rivalry

Chicago, Illinois, and Green Bay, Wisconsin, could not be more different in terms of size, cultural expanse, and historical detail. They are a little more than 200 miles apart, but seemingly worlds removed from each other in terms of style and substance.

But the two communities have one thing in common—they love their NFL team. And the people in those communities are bonded by a hatred of the other community's NFL team.

Ask a Bears fan about the Packers, and you will hear stories about back-hills behavior, small-town oddities, and basic stupidity. Ask a Packers fan about the Bears and you will hear derisive comments about the sins of the big city and basic stupidity. The jokes told by one fan base about the other are hilarious, and range from silly to shameless.

The source of all this hatred is time. The Bears and Packers have been playing against each other since 1921, and between the two franchises they have 22 NFL championships. The Packers lead the title count with 13, and have had much more success in the Super Bowl era with four titles to just one for the Bears, but the Bears have long held the lead in head-to-head wins, largely due to their supremacy in the 1940s and 1950s, when they won 30 of 41 contests.

At the beginning of the rivalry, the Bears were headed by coach and owner George Halas and the Packers were led by legendary coach Vince Lombardi, whose name prompts true reverence in all of Wisconsin. The NFL's title trophy is named after Lombardi, and the George Halas Trophy goes to the NFC champion. The relationship between Halas and Lombardi stoked the atmosphere that exists in the rivalry. Their names remain two of the most significant in NFL history, and are often spoken at the same time. Neither might have succeeded without the push from the other.

Almost 90 years after the rivalry started, when Lovie Smith became coach of the Bears, he declared his No. 1 goal for the team was to beat the Packers. Smith had no connection to the Bears before he was hired, but he knew his No. 1 job was to best the hated rivals from the north.

The Green Bay Packers were awarded their first NFL championship in 1929, when there was no championship game and the winner was declared based on won-loss record. The Packers won it again in 1930 and '31. Stopping the streak was the Bears, who won the title in 1932, their first under the Bears banner (the Chicago Staleys won the American Professional Football Association title in 1921).

Between 1933 and 1946, the Bears and Packers combined for eight NFL titles (the Bears had five of those). From 1961 to 1967, the Packers won the NFL title five times, including three in a row in 1965, '66, and '67. The Bears won the 1963 title to break up the Packers' hold on the championship.

In the '70s, both teams managed to win four straight games in the series. But starting with a Monday night victory in October of 1985, when the Bears were on their march to the Super Bowl, the Bears won eight consecutive games in the rivalry.

The Packers returned the favor in the 1990s, when they won 10 straight games, three times before a national Monday night audience.

Then, from November 22, 1992, to January 2, 2005, the Packers won 21 out of 25 games in the series.

Almost every game in the series produces memorable moments, and the mere mention of the name of great Chicago Bears in Green Bay (Payton, Butkus, Ditka, McMahon) or legendary Green Bay Packers in Chicago (Nitschke, Starr, Favre) can stir negative emotions among the faithful.

No professional football rivalry has ever reached the level of the Bears-Packers rivalry. At first it was because of the time involved, and now it is because of all of the times since then.

8 The 1963 NFL Champion Bears

For most of today's Chicago Bears fandom, the team that matters most is the 1985 Chicago Bears, who won Super Bowl XX in huge fashion, 46–10, over the New England Patriots. Many of the players from that team maintain business or media relationships in the Chicago area. Some people kind of wish they would go away already.

But before the 1985 Bears, the most special team in Bears history was the 1963 NFL champion Bears, led by longtime coach and owner George Halas on the sidelines and the likes of Bill George, Mike Ditka, and Doug Atkins on the field.

The 1963 Bears were 11–1–2 in the regular season (back when ties happened with more frequency than today) to win the Western Conference title, then defeated the New York Giants, led by famed quarterback Y.A. Tittle, 14–10, in the title game. The championship was the eighth in Chicago Bears history and the last for Halas.

In 1963, the Bears were 17 years removed from their last title. The hated Green Bay Packers were coming off back-to-back NFL titles. Memories of championship football in Chicago were fading.

The Bears were in the midst of a key coaching change that year, replacing aging defensive coach Clark Shaughnessy with an up-and-coming coach named George Allen (who would eventually become one of the most influential head coaches in the history of the NFL). Shaughnessy was the man who had installed the T-formation into the Bears' playbook years previous, but had been assigned the defense for several years prior to leaving the team in a disagreement with Halas.

The new defensive coordinator installed a 4-3 defense led by the line play of Hall of Famer Doug Atkins, a remarkably athletic defensive end who had a nose for getting to the quarterback. His partner on the other end of the defensive line was a younger player named Ed O'Bradovich.

Behind that line was a linebacking corps led by Hall of Fame linebacker Bill George, who was the first in a long line of incredible middle linebackers to play for the Bears. Atkins and O'Bradovich were the starting defensive ends, responsible for upsetting opposing quarterbacks into throwing the ball toward George.

On offense, the Bears were led by quarterback Bill Wade, a precision passer who came over from the Los Angeles Rams because of assistant coach George Allen. One of his main weapons was a young tight end named Mike Ditka, who was Rookie of the Year in 1961. Johnny Morris, a longtime civic hero in Chicago, had been converted from running back to flanker, a position that allowed him to be used in both the running game and passing game.

In the 1962 season, the Bears had been embarrassed twice by the Packers by scores of 49–0 and 38–7. The Packers had won five straight games in the greatest rivalry in football. But in the first game of the 1963 season, the Bears won in Green Bay 10–3 in a far more defensive game than had been played the previous year.

The Bears won four more games before losing at San Francisco, the only blemish on their record. They then won four more games, including a 26–7 win against Green Bay at Wrigley Field, before playing to consecutive 17–17 ties against Pittsburgh and Minnesota. They avenged the loss against San Francisco with a 27–7 win at Wrigley Field, and finished the regular season with a win over Detroit; a decision they needed to win the Western Conference title over the Packers. The Bears had two weeks to prepare to play the Eastern Conference title winners, the New York Giants.

The Giants themselves were a story. They had lost four of the previous five NFL title games. Their last title was in 1956 with a 47–7 shellacking of the Bears. Tittle had set an NFL record in 1963 by throwing for 36 touchdown passes.

The title game was played at Wrigley Field on December 29, 1963. It was a cold day, with temperatures in the single digits. Commissioner Pete Rozelle tried to get the game moved to Soldier Field because its seating capacity was much greater than that of Wrigley Field and it had lights, but he could not get the Bears to agree.

The Bears won the game 14–10. They trailed 10–7 at halftime but did not allow the Giants to score in the second half and won the game on a one-yard touchdown run by Wade. The Bears intercepted Tittle five times in the game.

9 Bronko Nagurski

Admit it: "Bronko Nagurski" is the best football name ever.

As it turned out, Bronko Nagurski was also one of the best football players of the first half of the 20th century.

Bronko Nagurski played for the Bears on two different occasions: from 1930 to 1937, when the Bears won two NFL titles, and then again in 1943, coming back to the team during World War II to help it win the 1943 crown.

Nagurski played fullback and linebacker, an indication of just how tough the man was. The position of fullback in those days required both running and throwing, and Nagurski threw a pair of touchdown passes to help the Bears win the 1933 NFL title against the New York Giants.

But Nagurski's story started way before he met George Halas and began playing for the Bears.

Nagurski was born in Canada of Polish-Ukrainian parents. The family moved to International Falls, Minnesota, where he worked in the timber industry in his teens, which allowed him to build his young muscular frame.

Nagurski played defensive tackle and fullback for the University of Minnesota Golden Gophers from 1927 to 1929. In his senior year, he led the nation in rushing and was named to every All-America team at fullback and some All-America teams as a defensive tackle.

With the Bears, Nagurski played both ways, and he succeeded in part because he simply was bigger and stronger than the players he played against. He stood 6'2", weighed around 225 pounds, and had power in his lower legs and upper body that allowed him to run over anyone in his path.

The 1932 NFL championship game was played indoors at the Chicago Stadium on an 80-yard field due to bad weather outdoors. The Bears beat the Portsmouth Spartans 9–0 in that game, and Nagurski threw a touchdown pass on what today would be called a halfback option, as he faked toward the line of scrimmage, then dropped back to throw the pass to halfback Red Grange for the touchdown. It was called a "jump pass" in the day, and the Spartans argued that it was illegal because Nagurski had not dropped back five yards as was required, but it still counted.

Nagurski retired from football in 1937, but was urged back to the Bears in 1943 as the war raged on. He scored a touchdown in the championship game that season and won his third NFL title.

Nagurski also had a career as a professional wrestler. He competed in the National Wrestling Association and won the world title in 1939.

The stories of Nagurski's talent and strength are numerous, but the best one is probably more fable than legend. According to the story, Nagurski scored a touchdown against the Washington Redskins at Wrigley Field by plowing through half the Redskins defense on the way to the end zone. So focused and powerful was he in his touchdown run that he did not stop until he ran into the brick wall of Wrigley Field's outfield. Upon returning to the huddle for the extra point, Nagurski supposedly said, "That last guy hit me awfully hard."

There are always players who stand out in their own time, but Nagurski's legendary status went beyond the 1930s and '40s. Well into the 21st century, Nagurski is considered one of the best college and professional football players of all time.

Nagurski has been honored in numerous ways, and the city of International Falls considers him the most beloved of their citizens. There is a Bronko Nagurski museum there, and the high school mascot is the Broncos.

Today, the Bronko Nagurski Trophy goes to the best defensive player in college football ever year, awarded and named by the Football Writers Association of America. That name was given to the trophy in 1993, 50 years after Nagurski retired from football, another indication of just how impressive the memory of his playing days remains.

10 T-formation

At some point in the 1930s, American football changed. After years of seeing the football snapped directly to a running back, teams began to use the quarterback for the purposes of deciding just what would happen with the football.

Early in the history of football, the ball was snapped from the center to a halfback or running back, who would try to find a hole in the line to get through. The quarterback was more of a blocking back.

Then came the innovation, in which the ball was snapped to the quarterback. What he did with it depended on how the other players were placed on the field prior to the snap.

The next step in the development of offensive football came in what is known as the T-formation. It was such a singular factor in the success of the Bears in the 1940s (when they won four championships) that it is mentioned in the team's fight song, "Bear Down, Chicago Bears."

"We'll never forget the way you thrilled the nation with your T-formation."

Clark Shaughnessy was a longtime football coach, and in the mid-1930s coached at the University of Chicago. While there,

Clyde Emrich

George Halas was an old-time football coach and a tough negotiator. But he was also an innovator.

In 1963, Halas hired former Olympic weightlifter Clyde Emrich to work with some of his players, developing their musculature with the use of resistance training. In 1971, Emrich became a full-time member of the staff, one of the first full-time strength coaches in the NFL.

Emrich competed in the 1952 Olympic Games, finishing eighth in his weight class. His best world competition finishes were a gold medal in the 1959 Pan American Games in Chicago and a second in the 1955 World Championships in Munich.

Emrich worked for the Bears until 1991, then was asked back in the mid-2000s. In 2008, the Bears named their weight room after Emrich.

he became friendly with Bears owner George Halas, and the two worked together to install Shaughnessy's version of the T-formation into the Bears attack. When the Bears beat the Washington Redskins 73–0 in the 1940 NFL Championship Game, it was the T-formation that was given the credit.

The initial T-formation looked from above just like a "T," with the extended offensive line on top, which would have seven players, a quarterback behind center, and three running backs lined up horizontally as the bottom slightly extended line of the "T." Based on the call made by the coach or quarterback, those three running backs would move, serving either as blockers or ballcarriers, and the quarterback not only would have three options in terms of running plays, but the defense would have three running attacks to try to prepare for.

Once teams figured out all of the opportunities they had in handing the ball off in a T-formation, their next possibility was to call an option play, which is where the quarterback fakes the handoff to get the defense moving in one direction, then runs a sweep himself right or left with the intent of passing. With three running backs coming out of the backfield, plus receivers that were already at the line of scrimmage, the quarterback had more options than defenses had answers.

Sid Luckman, the Brooklyn-born quarterback out of Columbia University, came to the Bears with the intellect needed to run the T-formation. He actually failed in his first attempt to run the offense, which had so many different attack points that it was a bit complicated. But he understood it midway through his first season with the Bears in 1939 and became the most effective quarterback in Bears history.

Football coaches today will tell you that any offensive formation that includes at least one running back standing behind the quarterback, who is under center, is a variation of the T-formation.

11 Bears in the Hall of Fame

As of February 2020, the Chicago Bears had the most players enshrined in the Pro Football Hall of Fame, with 30. That is counting only the players who spent a majority, if not all, of their career with the Bears. Bears fans are proud to tell you the Green Bay Packers only have 25.

The list starts, appropriately enough, with coach and player George Halas, who remains such a figure in Bears history that even three decades after his death, the team still wears a football-shaped patch on their uniforms with his initials: GSH. Halas' association with the Bears began in 1920, but there were other players from the 1920s that ended up in the Hall of Fame: Red Grange, Ed

Healey, Link Lyman, George Trafton, and player and coach Paddy Driscoll.

In the 1930s, when the Bears won championships in 1932 and 1933, they had eventual Hall of Famers in Dan Fortmann, Bill Hewitt, star quarterback Sid Luckman, George Musso, Bronko Nagurski, and Joe Stydahar.

Hall of Famers That Don't Count

There are 28 players in the Pro Football Hall of Fame who spent a majority, if not the entirety, of their career with the Bears. But there are five Hall of Famers who spent a year or two with the Bears, and don't count on the Bears' list of contributors.

Tops among those who played a short while for the Bears are quarterback Bobby Layne and defensive lineman Alan Page. Layne was actually drafted by the Bears in the 1948 NFL Draft, third overall, but the Bears had an embarrassment of quarterback talent at the time. Sid Luckman, the best quarterback in Bears history, and Johnny Lujack, who did an admirable job following Luckman, were on the team in 1948, and Layne played only one season before the Bears traded him to Detroit.

While with the Lions, Layne actually led the team to three NFL championships (yes, the Lions did win championships once upon a time). He played 15 years of pro football, and if he had stayed with the Bears, he might have been the franchise's greatest quarterback instead of Luckman. We will never know.

Page played in the NFL from 1967 to 1981, but played his first 12 seasons with the Minnesota Vikings, where he had a Hall of Fame career that included four NFC championships and, unfortunately for the Vikings, no Super Bowl wins. He was Defensive Player of the Year for either the NFC or the NFL numerous times.

He joined the Bears during the 1978 season and led the team in sacks in his first campaign, getting to the quarterback 11½ times. He was credited with 40 sacks (unofficial totals) in his four seasons with the Bears.

Page eventually went on to be an Associate Justice on the Minnesota Supreme Court. He was inducted into the Pro Football Hall of Fame in 1988.

With Luckman at the helm, the Bears won four championships in the 1940s ('40, '41, '43, and '46) and had players like George Blanda, George Connor, George McAfee, and Clyde "Bulldog" Turner, all who ended up in the Hall of Fame.

Between 1946 and 1963, the Bears went without titles, but they still had legendary players like Doug Atkins, Bill George, and Stan Jones who entered the Hall of Fame (all three also played on the '63 championship team).

In the 1960s, the Bears had only one title team, in 1963, but they had several Hall of Fame players on the roster, some of them names that remained in the city's memory banks for decades, including tight end (and eventual head coach) Mike Ditka, linebacker Dick Butkus, and running back Gale Sayers.

In 1974, Jim Finks joined the team as general manager, and in 1975 he drafted Walter Payton out of Jackson State University. They both became members of the Pro Football Hall of Fame.

The 1980s mattered because they produced the only Super Bowl champion—perhaps the greatest team of all time—in the 1985 Bears. Hall of Fame players on that club besides Payton were defensive tackle Dan Hampton, defensive end Richard Dent, middle linebacker Mike Singletary, and the only other Hall of Fame offensive player on the squad, tackle Jimbo Covert.

Between the Super Bowl of 1985 and the Super Bowl appearance in 2006, only one player stood out enough to garner Hall of Fame selection—linebacker Brian Urlacher.

By position, the Bears have just three quarterbacks (with Sid Luckman the last, who ended his playing career in 1950), four running backs, one receiver (Ditka, who was actually a tight end), nine offensive linemen, seven defensive linemen, six linebackers, and only one defensive secondary player (George McAfee) in the Hall of Fame. Because players in the first half of the 20th century played both ways, the total comes out to more than 30.

Also, George Halas and Paddy Driscoll were players and coaches. Throw in Mike Ditka, and three former Bears coaches are in the Hall of Fame.

12 NFL's Top 100

The National Football League declared the 2019 season to be the 100th anniversary of the league, dating back to the start of professional football, which began in Dayton, Ohio, in September 1920.

To celebrate the anniversary, the NFL enlisted two dozen experts, including coaches, team executives, former players, and members of the media, to determine the top 100 players in league history. They ended up selecting 12 running backs, 10 quarterbacks, 10 wide receivers, seven tackles, seven guards, seven defensive ends, seven defensive tackles, seven cornerbacks, six outside linebackers, six middle/inside linebackers, six safeties, five tight ends, four centers, two kickers, two punters, and two kick/punt returners. They also selected 10 all-time great coaches.

The Chicago Bears were one of the teams that played in that first season, although they were the Chicago Staleys at the time. With 100 years of history to count on, it's not surprising that the Bears ended up with seven players and one coach on the list of top 100 players.

What is also not surprising is that they did not get anyone on the list of 10 quarterbacks. Several chapters of this book explain why. (The Bears also had no wide receivers, and only three defensive players).

Here are the players selected as part of the NFL's Top 100 (each of these players is mentioned multiple times in other chapters):

Coach—George Halas. Halas effectively created the NFL. He may have been the first person selected to any of the positions on the list.

Running back—Ask someone which position on the field the Bears would have double representation on the NFL's Top 100 players, and you would probably hear many "linebacker" responses. Instead, Walter Payton and Gale Sayers were among the 12 running backs selected to the team. From 1965 to 1987, the Bears had one of the most powerful running games in the league.

Guard—Dan Fortmann, who came from Colgate University to play eight seasons with the Bears and won three NFL championships.

Tight end—Mike Ditka came from the University of Pittsburgh and reinvented the tight end position as an offensive threat under the guidance of Halas. He played only six seasons for the Bears, but without him, the position might not have ended up with four other tight ends on the list.

Middle linebacker—Dick Butkus was a local hero from Vocational High School in Chicago to the University of Illinois to the Bears. He ended up earning eight Pro Bowl appearances, and like Ditka, Butkus was considered the man who invented the middle linebacker position.

Defensive end—Bill Hewitt came out of the University of Michigan and played five seasons with the Bears in the 1930s, winning two NFL championships. He is best known as one of the last players in the league to play without a helmet.

Kick returner—From the University of Miami, Devin Hester was drafted as a wide receiver but made his name as a kick returner. He was spectacular at the position and scored on the opening kickoff of Super Bowl XLI.

Arguments over the NFL Top 100 will go on forever. How many Bears do you think are missing from this list?

13 Brian Urlacher

The legacy of middle linebackers on the Chicago Bears dates back to the 1940s when Bill George danced between the defensive line and the second line of defense. Dick Butkus brought a brutality to the position that remained a characteristic of the team for decades. Mike Singletary's desire to succeed and single-minded purpose brought a focus to a defense that eventually won a Super Bowl.

In 2000, upon all of that history came a converted safety out of New Mexico named Brian Urlacher, who was again able to redefine the position of middle linebacker with a previously unseen amount of athleticism. He had speed reserved for, well, defensive backs, and a nose for the ball that produced numerous turnovers, which also then produced numerous touchdowns.

Urlacher played multiple sports in high school, and in college he played on both sides of the ball. Because he possessed the speed and hand-eye coordination of a defensive back and the physique of a linebacker, his college coach transformed the Lobos defense to suit his abilities. Urlacher finished his college career at New Mexico as the most decorated player in the school's football history.

The Bears drafted Urlacher ninth overall in the 2000 NFL Draft. The team had suffered through its fourth losing season in a row. The franchise had also lost one of its favorite sons when Walter Payton passed away late in 1999.

Because of his speed and athleticism, Bears coach Dick Jauron installed the rookie Urlacher at strong-side linebacker for his first game. Urlacher did not play well in that game, and did not start his second NFL game. Before the third game, veteran middle linebacker Barry Minter got injured, and Urlacher stepped in to start. He played the rest of that season and the next 12 as the Bears'

Brian Urlacher celebrating after stopping Michael Vick, who wasn't used to being caught by linebackers.

middle linebacker. Urlacher was the 2000 NFL Defensive Rookie of the Year. Unleashed by the defensive teachings of new head coach Lovie Smith when he replaced Dick Jauron to start the 2004 season, Urlacher became the NFL Defensive Player of the Year in 2005.

Urlacher's most famous game occurred in the Super Bowl–bound 2006 season in the new University of Phoenix Stadium in Glendale, Arizona, home to the Arizona Cardinals. On Monday night, October 16, the Bears took a flashy 5–0 record to the desert and were expected to feast on the Cardinals. But a series of circumstances on both offense and defense turned the game into a potential embarrassment as the home team had a 20–0 halftime lead.

Then something happened, to Urlacher and his legacy. After the Bears got one touchdown off a defensive fumble recovery, Urlacher took it upon himself to get the ball back for the Bears by simply taking the ball out of the hands of Arizona running back Edgerrin James. Urlacher did not maintain possession of the ball; instead it ended up in the hands of cornerback Charles Tillman, who scored the second defensive touchdown of the half for the Bears. They won the game when return specialist Devin Hester scored on an 83-yard punt return. Urlacher ended the game with 25 tackles, and that performance before a national television audience cemented his status.

Through the 2012 season, Urlacher had made the Pro Bowl eight times. He was an official All-Pro five times. But injuries took their toll on Urlacher, who began to slow down after the Super Bowl. Arthritis in his back, a dislocated wrist (that caused him to miss an entire season), and a sprained MCL affected his performance, although he occasionally turned in massive defensive games when he felt right.

He announced his retirement in May 2013 and was inducted into the NFL Hall of Fame in 2018.

14 The 46 Defense

The 46 defense was designed by former Bears defensive coordinator Buddy Ryan and run to perfection by the group of players considered to be arguably the best defense in the history of the NFL.

While Ryan first developed his unique defensive philosophy while working with the New York Jets of the old American Football League, the 46 defense was solidified when he joined the Bears after working as the defensive line coach for the Minnesota Vikings. The defense was built on a 4-3 scheme upfront, with four down linemen and three linebackers, with four defensive backs behind.

There is no "6" in the design of the defense. The "46" moniker came from the jersey number of the hardest hitting player on the Bears at the time Ryan showed up in 1979, safety Doug Plank.

The 46 defense started at the defensive line, which was assigned to distract and dismay the quarterback at all times. The players were aware when the quarterback made a handoff to a running back, and did a fine job stopping that as well, but their first job was to get to the quarterback, or force him to be uncomfortable enough to leave the pocket.

Ryan assigned the defensive line to shift toward the weak side of the offensive line. If the offense is playing one tight end, creating a strong side for the run, the defensive line shifts toward the weak side to create mismatches and fill gaps. At the same time, the linebackers would shift to the strong side to protect against the run.

While creating unusual player pairings between the offensive and defensive lines, the 46 also caused the offense to reconsider its plans at the line of scrimmage. The quarterback had to concern himself with an attack from his weak side, while trying to determine whether to send his running back into the strong-side defense that included two linebackers specifically assigned to stop the run.

All of this defensive scheming was predicated on the belief that the cornerbacks could handle receivers in man coverage, and the safeties were fast enough to show blitz on occasion and then drop back into coverage when required to do so. Basically, the 46 defense needed tremendous athletes, and Ryan had them in 1985.

The defensive line had William "the Refrigerator" Perry and Steve McMichael as the tackles and Richard Dent and Dan Hampton as the defensive ends. Perry weighed 335 pounds during the championship year, McMichael was agile and a little bit crazy, and Dent and Hampton were tall and strong. Dent and Hampton, both at 6'5", were difficult to pass against because of their height.

The linebackers were the next weapon, and they were centered by the extremely intense Mike Singletary, who was actually a bit small as middle linebackers go but was very mobile. Wilber Marshall was the weak-side linebacker and Otis Wilson was the strong-side linebacker.

The safeties were Gary Fencik and Dave Duerson, and the cornerbacks were Mike Richardson and Leslie Frazier.

15 Lovie Smith

After Mike Ditka left the Bears, they had a couple of coaches who failed to reach a level of success that would allow them to stay in the position for long. Dave Wannstedt (1993–1998) and Dick

Jauron (1999–2003) were the kind of coaches team president Michael McCaskey was expected to hire, although the Bears did attract a great deal of attention by corralling Wannstedt, who was a Dallas Cowboys assistant and much sought after for a first-time head coaching position.

Both Wannstedt and Jauron managed to earn Coach of the Year honors (Wannstedt was UPI's choice in 1994, Jauron was the AP choice in 2001) for getting the Bears into the playoffs once. But those successes were followed by non-playoff years and neither man managed to stay for too long.

So in 2004 the Bears were looking for a new head coach. They were almost certain to choose another assistant coach to give him his first head coaching position.

The Bears selected St. Louis Rams defensive coordinator Lovie Smith, who became the first African American head coach for the Bears. He served as coach from 2004 to 2012, and got the Bears to one Super Bowl appearance, in which they lost to the Indianapolis Colts at the end of the 2006 season.

Since George Halas first played for and coached the Chicago Staleys in 1920, there were 12 coaches for the Bears prior to Smith being hired (Halas only counts once although he coached the team four different times). Of those 12, Smith ranked third in longevity behind Halas and Mike Ditka.

Lovie Smith (and yes, that is his real first name) moved from his last of numerous college assistant coaching jobs at Ohio State to join Tony Dungy on the staff of the Tampa Bay Buccaneers as linebacker coach. Dungy and Smith combined their knowledge of defense to create what became known as the Tampa 2 defense, which was credited for the success the Buccaneers had while the two men worked together.

At the end of the 2001 season, Dungy was fired from the Buccaneers, and Smith was looking for work. He was hired as defensive coordinator of the St. Louis Rams, effectively serving as the assistant head coach for Mike Martz, the offensive-minded leader of the Rams. With the Greatest Show on Turf on offense and the successful use of the Tampa 2 defense, the Rams got to Super Bowl XXXVI after the 2001 season and lost to the New England Patriots.

Upon his arrival in Chicago, Smith drew attention with his Texas drawl; his slow, considerate manner of speaking; and his announced goals, the first of which was to beat the Green Bay Packers on a regular basis.

Smith was the head coach of the defense for the Bears, and handed the offensive duties off to numerous offensive coordinators over the years, including his former boss, Mike Martz. But the Bears offense could never match the Bears defense in terms of success or firepower.

Smith was the ultimate player's coach. He never said a bad word about his players publicly; he was assailed frequently in the press for failing to provide adequate information on injuries and depth-chart changes. A fiercely private man, he made little effort to let the public know much about him, which made him similar to his predecessor, Dick Jauron, but flew in the face of the behavior of Chicago's favorite coach, Mike Ditka.

The Bears made early progress under Smith. His first season they were 5–11, but that was followed by an 11–5 season and an appearance in the playoffs (where they lost to the Carolina Panthers). In 2006 the Bears were 13–3, had one of the most dominant defenses in the NFL in years, and advanced to Super Bowl XLI, where they lost to the Indianapolis Colts.

Following that season, Smith got a new four-year contract, signaling the team's pleasure with his success. However, he allowed the team to let go of his defensive coordinator, Ron Rivera, who was also a very popular member of the first Super Bowl team in 1985, on which he'd been a backup linebacker. Rivera had helped Smith build the defense that led the Bears to Super Bowl XLI, and the decision to remove him was seen as a power play on Smith's part. It was not well received publicly.

Over the next seasons, despite still having a powerful and opportunistic defense, the Bears made the playoffs only once, in 2010, when they lost the hated Packers in the NFC Championship Game. When the Bears failed to make the playoffs after the 2012 season, despite starting the season 7–1, Smith was fired.

Oddly, Smith eventually was hired to his first college head coaching position in 2016 at the University of Illinois, which is where legendary Bears player and coach George Halas played his college ball.

16 1986 (the Year After)

The Super Bowl XX victory was the greatest moment in modern Bears history, and has remained so well into the 21st century. But it came with some pain for Bears fans, because it was not followed by a Super Bowl XXI victory, or any subsequent championships.

Ask anyone who was there, and they will tell you the Bears were so dominant in 1985 they should have been able to pile up at least one other NFL title. Instead, they flamed out in the playoffs in 1986.

The season started in spectacular fashion, as the Bears took their popularity on the road, playing in the first American Bowl in famed Wembley Stadium in London, England. The Bears beat the Dallas Cowboys 17–6 in that contest.

Any concern that the trip to London would be a distraction turned out to be unfounded. The Bears actually had an extremely successful 1986 season before they got to the playoffs.

When the 1986 season started, another Super Bowl appearance seemed secure, and the Bears played almost as strongly as they did the previous season. In fact, from a statistical standpoint, the Bears were better than they were in 1985. The 1986 Bears set an NFL record for least amount of points scored against, a total of 187 in 16 games (the 1985 team had allowed 198 points).

The Bears went 14–2 in 1986, only one game worse than in 1985. Their losses were to the Minnesota Vikings and Los Angeles Rams in midseason. Their 14–2 record was the best in the league, tied with the New York Giants.

The 1985 Bears had been remarkably healthy all season long. The 1986 Bears did not have the same luck. Quarterback Jim McMahon, who came to camp overweight after enjoying the Super Bowl success, missed six of the first 12 games due to injury. After Game 12, he was done for the season.

In that 12th game, against the Green Bay Packers, McMahon was injured on one of the most infamous plays in Bears history. Packers defensive lineman Charles Martin grabbed McMahon well after a pass play, picked him up, and slammed him to the ground like one might do if he was angry with his teddy bear. McMahon suffered a separated shoulder and was out for the season.

The Bears struggled to find a replacement for McMahon, giving the job alternatively to Mike Tomczak, Steve Fuller, and eventually Doug Flutie, the popular but diminutive quarterback from Boston College.

The Bears actually entered the playoffs with a full head of steam. Including the Packers game in which McMahon was injured, the Bears won their final seven games, giving up no more than 14 points in any contest.

The Bears had a first-round bye thanks to their stellar record and entered the divisional playoff game against the Washington Redskins as the favorite. But the Bears gave up 20 points in the second half of that game, and lost 27–13. The dream of a second Super Bowl title was gone.

17 Dick Butkus

Having seen the invention of the middle linebacker in the career of Bill George, the Bears got extremely lucky when they drafted Butkus, a Chicago-born-and-raised local hero who stayed close to home and played his college ball at the University of Illinois.

Butkus, different from George in body type, was a powerful, sturdy, and unrelenting football player, a true believer in the use of physical strength and desire to overcome opponents. In the history of the NFL, no player was more feared by opponents than Butkus.

Throughout his playing career, Butkus was known as the most feared man in football. If you need proof, just find a copy of the 1970 *Sports Illustrated* which has a picture of Butkus on the cover with the words "Most Feared Man in the Game."

Butkus was raised on the south side of Chicago and made a name for himself playing football at Chicago Vocational High School. He enrolled at the University of Illinois in 1961 and played football for the Illini from 1962 to 1964. In 1963, the team won the Big Ten title, and Butkus led the team that season with 145 tackles. The team finished third in the Associated Press rankings that season.

He played both ways, settling in as center on the offensive side of the ball and linebacker on defense. He received numerous awards for his college playing performances, including the American Football Coaches Association Player of the Year Award for 1964.

Dick Butkus informs the official that he disagrees with his call.

Despite having no offensive stats to show, he finished third in the Heisman Trophy balloting in 1964.

The Bears selected Butkus third in the 1965 NFL Draft, getting that selection in a trade with the Pittsburgh Steelers. With the next pick in the draft, No. 4 in the first round, the Bears selected running back Gale Sayers out of the University of Kansas. Sayers and Butkus finished first and second in NFL Rookie of the Year honors in their first season.

When the Bears drafted Butkus, they already had an established middle linebacker named Bill George, who had all but invented the position in the 1950s. George said he recognized Butkus' ability in his first practice.

"The second I saw him on the field [at training camp] I knew my playing days were over," George said. "Nobody ever looked that good before or since." George played with Butkus that 1965 season.

Butkus, who was 6'3" and 245 pounds, led a defense that struggled to keep the team in games. He played for nine seasons, before knee injuries forced him out in 1973. During his nine years, the Bears had just two winning seasons and never made the playoffs. The team's best finish with Butkus on the roster was in his rookie season, when they went 9–5.

Linebacker stats are a little hard to come by, but when he retired, Butkus had the NFL record for opponent fumbles recovered at 25.

Butkus suffered a strained relationship with the Bears for a few years when he sued the team over improper treatment of his injuries and the team's insistence that he play despite being injured. Those feelings remained until owner George Halas died in 1983. After that, Butkus renewed his relationship with the club and even did some radio work for the team.

But it wasn't on the radio where Butkus would make his post-NFL career. He made dozens of appearances in film and TV, sometimes playing a football player, sometimes portraying himself. But he had a relatively successful TV show titled *My Two Dads,* and the best movie of his list of film appearances might have been the football film *Any Given Sunday.*

Another Butkus, Dick's nephew Luke, played football at Illinois and worked for the Bears as offensive line coach in 2007.

Butkus and former Bears running back Red Grange are the only two players to have their jersey number retired by the University of Illinois. Their numbers with the Bears were retired as well, and they are both in the Pro Football Hall of Fame. Sayers and Butkus had their jersey numbers retired by the Bears on the same Monday night, October 31, 1994, when the Bears were playing the Green Bay Packers.

In 2019, Butkus was named one of the top 100 players in the NFL's 100-year history, and was one of 12 linebackers selected for that honor.

18 Monsters of the Midway

In the 1930s and 1940s, the Chicago Bears owned the NFL from a competitive standpoint. They won two titles in the 1930s and four more titles over seven seasons, starting in 1940 and ending in 1946.

Because of their dominance, and the fact that their star players and coach George Halas were such prominent national sports figures, the Bears were given the name "Monsters of the Midway," a name that stuck with the team despite long periods without titles. The name was revisited when the Bears became the most dominant team in the modern era of football on the way to the franchise's only Super Bowl win after the 1985 season.

The name itself was stolen, in a way. It had previously been used to describe the University of Chicago football team, and "the Midway" was a pleasant and large park area near the Hyde Park campus of U of C. The Midway Plaisance is a mile-long stretch of grassy park area that runs south of the University of Chicago campus. It was a major location of entertainment during the 1893 World's Columbian Exposition in Chicago. Today the word "Midway" is used as a center location for games of chance and carnival barkers. The Midway Plaisance still exists today.

The University of Chicago football program ended in 1939, leaving the name up for grabs. When the Bears started winning in such dominant fashion, it was an easy moniker to attach. The Bears were a powerful bunch at the time, and when legendary fullback and linebacker Bronko Nagurski came out of retirement to help the Bears claim the 1943 title, the "Monsters of the Midway" name stuck like glue.

Today, the name brings to mind the defensive powerhouse teams of the 1980s, which barely needed (or had) an offensive attack in order to win games. But the original Monsters of the Midway were an offensive powerhouse, which won the 1940 NFL title game 73–0 against the Washington Redskins, and the 1941 game by the score of 37–9 against the New York Giants. Of course, the 1985 Super Bowl score was 46–10 in favor of the Bears, so maybe the name applied both ways then, too.

Seemingly forever, defense has been the mainstay of the Bears' teams, and monsters are best served in football on the defensive side. When the Bears advanced to the Super Bowl after the 2006 season, and their only means of winning sometimes was through defensive strength, the "Monsters of the Midway" name was once again revisited.

19 2006 NFC Champions

Under new head coach Lovie Smith, the Bears were on the rise in the middle of the first decade of the new century. After going 5–11 in 2004, his first season, Smith and the staunch Bears defense won the NFC North by flipping their record to 11–5. Jumping off from there, the 2006 Bears went 13–3, the best record in the NFC, hosted both Seattle and the New Orleans Saints in the playoffs, and found themselves in the Super Bowl for the second time.

Like almost every other team the Bears ever had, the 2006 team was built on a strong defense. Led by middle linebacker Brian Urlacher, the team not only stopped the opposing offenses from scoring, often it did so simply by taking the ball away from them.

Smith prided himself on his coaching belief that a defense has to get takeaways, either through fumbles or interceptions. The 2006 team took that lesson to heart. The defensive lineup was so good and so memorable that fans could go player by player and list them all. The front line had Alex Brown, Tommie Harris, Tank Johnson, and Adewale Ogunleye. The linebackers were Lance Briggs, Brian Urlacher, and Hunter Hillenmeyer. The secondary was made up of Charles "Peanut" Tillman, Chris Harris, Danieal Manning, and Nathan Vasher. Rookie Mark Anderson provided an unexpected spark as a reserve DE and led the team with 12 sacks (a number he failed to match through the rest of his career with the Bears).

But the offense was questionable. Led by undersized quarterback Rex Grossman, the Bears had little in the way of an offensive attack. Veteran running back Thomas Jones shared time with second-year upstart Cedric Benson out of Texas. Veteran Muhsin Muhammad and stick-figure Bernard Berrian were the best of a poor receiving corps.

The Bears won their first seven games of the 2006 season, including the season-opening decision over the hated Green Bay Packers. Enthusiasm was ramped up as Bears fans hoped for a title run for the first time since the 1985 team cruised through the regular season and the Super Bowl.

On October 16, 2006, the Bears visited the Arizona Cardinals. At one point, the Cardinals franchise was in Chicago, before moving to St. Louis, before moving to Phoenix. The Cardinals did not figure to put up much of a battle for the suddenly emboldened Bears.

However, at halftime, the Cardinals had a 20–0 lead as the Bears offense, led by the extremely inconsistent Rex Grossman, could not produce points. After three quarters, the Cardinals still led 23–10, and the Bears' unbeaten season looked ready to end.

But, in a performance that stood as testament to the power of the defense, the Bears scored two defensive touchdowns quickly. Veteran safety Mike Brown picked up a Cardinal fumble and returned it three yards for a touchdown. Brian Urlacher forced a fumble that cornerback Charles Tillman picked up for another score. With the score 23–17 in favor of Arizona, rookie returner Devin Hester took a punt 83 yards for the go-ahead touchdown, and the Bears were still unbeaten and had proven that no lead was safe against the vaunted Bears defense.

The Bears' first loss that season came against the Miami Dolphins, which was seen as some sort of sign, since the 1985 Bears' only loss that season was against the Dolphins. But the Bears lost again three weeks later to the New England Patriots (the team the 1985 Bears beat in the Super Bowl), and the Bears ended the regular season with a New Year's Eve loss to the Green Bay Packers.

It was not a good sign that the Bears needed overtime to win the divisional round playoff game against the Seattle Seahawks at Soldier Field, 27–24. But they righted the ship against the New Orleans Saints the next weekend, winning 39–14 in a game played under cold and snowy conditions. The Bears had advanced to the Super Bowl for the first time since 1985, and everyone on the team was being hailed as heroes.

The Super Bowl was played at Dolphin Stadium in Miami and it rained from the first sight of light in the morning through to the end of the game late that Sunday night. The hope was that the bad weather would help the Bears compete against Peyton Manning and the high-powered Indianapolis Colts offense.

Hester opened Super Bowl XLI with a 92-yard return for a touchdown, giving the Bears an exciting and unexpected 7–0 lead. But the Bears could not contain the Colts, and Grossman failed miserably on the big stage, allowing the Colts to record a wet 29–17 victory in what turned out to be a boring and uneventful Super Bowl.

20 Super Bowl XLI

The Super Bowl played on February 4, 2007, between the Chicago Bears and the Indianapolis Colts had a long list of story lines. The game did not match the pregame hype.

Lovie Smith, coach of the Bears, and Tony Dungy, longtime coach of the Colts, were the first two African American coaches to lead teams in the Super Bowl. Dungy was a mentor to Smith, who worked under Dungy when they were employed by the Tampa Bay Buccaneers years earlier.

For Chicago, the game represented the chance to move on from the success of the 1985 team that won Super Bowl XX by the ridiculous score of 46–10 against the New England Patriots. A city that adored those '85 Bears was still looking for something else to fall in love with, and the 2006 Bears provided a glimmer of hope.

The Colts were playing in their first Super Bowl since moving from Baltimore in the early 1980s. They had been threatening to get to "the Dance" for years prior to 2006, and Colts quarterback Peyton Manning was battling a reputation for being not quite good enough to win the big game.

The game was played at Dolphin Stadium in Miami. After a week of beautiful, warm weather, the clouds rolled in Saturday night and by Sunday morning a steady drizzle had begun. The entire game was played in rain, mostly a constant nagging presence but occasionally a heavy downpour.

The Bears entered the game as a touchdown underdog. They were known for their powerful defense, led by linebacker Brian Urlacher and defensive linemen Adewale Ogunleye and Tommie Harris. They were saddled by their inconsistent offense, led by problematic quarterback Rex Grossman.

The Bears offense that season was so limited that the best chances the Bears had to score most games was either by the defense coming up with a turnover that turned into a touchdown or waiting for the other team to kick to them.

In 2006, Devin Hester was a rookie return man out of the University of Miami. He was a second-round pick, and certainly an iffy one at that. Although his playing position at Miami was as a cornerback, he was going to make his mark in the NFL as a return man, and make his mark he did.

Hester had six touchdowns in 2006, two off kickoffs, three off punts, and one for 108 yards when the New York Giants made the mistake of trying to kick a field goal on a very windy day at Giants Stadium in East Rutherford, New Jersey, and Hester caught the short kick deep in the end zone and returned it to the other end zone for one of the most spectacular touchdowns in the history of the NFL.

Until that night in Miami, that is. On the opening kickoff by the Colts, Hester ran the ball back 92 yards for a touchdown, giving the Bears the earliest score in the history of the Super Bowl. What was so remarkable about that feat is that anyone who watched that game will tell you they fully expected Hester to score that touchdown.

So the Bears, touchdown underdogs going into the game, were a touchdown up after about 10 seconds. Things looked good for the Bears minutes later when Chris Harris intercepted a Manning pass as the Bears defense indicated its intentions to give the Bears every chance to win.

The Colts scored on a 53-yard touchdown pass from Manning to Reggie Wayne but missed the extra point. Late in the first quarter, the Bears' offense finally showed up as veteran running back Thomas Jones, who battled upstart youngster Cedric Benson for playing time all season, ran the ball 53 yards down to the Colts 4-yard line, and Grossman completed a touchdown pass to Muhsin Muhammad for a shocking 14–6 Bears lead.

The Colts had a field goal and a touchdown in the second quarter to take a 16–14 halftime lead. The feeling at the break was that the Bears had given the Colts a battle for 30 minutes but would be hard-pressed to contain the Indianapolis offense in the second half or find some offense of their own.

Indianapolis kicker Adam Vinatieri, who had already won three Super Bowl rings previously with the New England Patriots, had a pair of third-quarter field goals to give the Colts a 22–14 lead. Robbie Gould of the Bears came back with one of his own for a 22–17 difference going into the fourth quarter.

But with the rain dampening the spirits of almost everyone involved, the Colts captured the game early in the fourth quarter when cornerback Kelvin Hayden intercepted a Grossman pass and returned it 56 yards for the game's final score.

Grossman had not played a horrible game, completing 20 of 28 passes for 165 yards and a touchdown, but he had two interceptions as well. Jones ran for 112 yards as Benson suffered a knee injury in the first half of the game and did not return.

The Bears were hopeful they would return to the Super Bowl with the defense they had in place. After all, rookie Mark Anderson had recorded 12 sacks in his first season, and Urlacher and linebacker Lance Briggs were still in their prime. But Coach Smith could never solve the needs of the offense, Urlacher started getting hurt, and the Bears' fortunes never again matched that bright light of 2006 under Smith, who was fired after the 2012 season.

21 Red Grange

The first superstar the Bears ever had was Harold Edward "Red" Grange, a star running back at the University of Illinois.

Grange grew up in Pennsylvania but played his high school football in Wheaton, Illinois, where he was a four-star athlete. He went from Wheaton to the University of Illinois, where he played football and ran track. He won the state title in the long jump, high jump, and the 100-yard dash.

In 1924, Grange was at the height of his popularity as the star halfback for the Illini. Sportswriters in the day fumbled over each other trying to come up with ways to describe what Grange could do. Chicago sportswriter Walter Brown tabbed Grange as the "Galloping Ghost," a name that stuck with him into his professional career.

In 1923, Grange led Illinois to the national championship. In 1924, he scored five touchdowns against Michigan, four of them in the first 12 minutes of the game.

In 1925, the University of Illinois retired Grange's number 77. The only other number retired in Illini football history is the No. 50 belonging to former linebacker and future Bears middle linebacker Dick Butkus. Today, Grange is considered by some to be the greatest college football player of all time.

In 1925, there was no pro football draft for eligible college players. There were few eligibility rules at all. Players were recruited to join pro teams.

Bears owner George Halas wanted Grange, who was a local hero from his exploits in Champaign at U of I. So he concocted a plan with a businessman to offer Grange the unheard-of sum of $100,000 to join the Bears and participate in a bus tour of the country, showcasing his talents and the talents of the Bears. It was also to serve as a promotional vehicle for the young NFL.

Grange accepted Halas' offer, and the tour was a huge success. Sportswriters from around the country came to know of Grange's abilities, and the football league was spurred on by the notice gained from the tour and two subsequent follow-up events.

After playing for the Bears in five games in 1925, Grange got into a disagreement with Halas over money and formed his own league, called the American Football League, with his manager, C.C. Pyle. He played for the New York Yankees for two seasons, the second in the NFL after the AFL folded and the Yankees joined the league.

In 1929, Grange returned to the Bears, but he had suffered a significant injury in his second season with the Yankees (playing against the Bears), and was nowhere near as dangerous a runner in his subsequent years. Still, he scored eight touchdowns for the Bears in 1930 and seven more in 1931. In 1932, Grange caught a pass from Bronko Nagurski which he turned into a touchdown to win the NFL title that year. He also won a title with the 1933 Bears and played a final year in 1934 before retiring.

Grange served as the Bears' radio announcer for several years in the 1950s.

22 Practice Facilities

George Halas changed professional football in so many ways. His $100,000 contract to Red Grange upped the ante for top players. He brought the T-formation to the pro game. He assisted in the creation of the middle linebacker position.

In 1933, Halas had another innovation. He shipped his team to the University of Notre Dame for training camp, rather than have them practice in the Chicago area.

Over the years, the Bears moved from Indiana to Wisconsin to Indiana to Wisconsin before settling in at a school in Central Illinois for their summer training homes. In some places, you can still see what life was like for the Bears if you visit the schools they used as summer homes.

The idea of taking teams away from home for training camp is one that baseball teams use with their spring training in Florida and Arizona. While baseball does it for weather reasons, football does it more for team building; the idea is to have players living with each other in a more personal setting, allowing them to get to know each other and concentrate on football rather than on home issues.

The Bears used Notre Dame for just that one season, then moved to the football field at Lane Tech High School for training camp in 1934. In 1935, the Bears moved again, this time to St. John's Military Academy in Delafield, Wisconsin.

In 1944, the Bears signed a contract with St. Joseph's College in Rensselaer, Indiana, to use its facilities during a six-week period in July and August to train for the upcoming season. St. Joseph's is a two-hour drive from Chicago, a short enough drive to get home when necessary but far enough away to create an atmosphere of camaraderie. There is a residence hall at St. Joseph's named for George Halas in honor of the team's time at the school.

The Bears continued their association with St. Joseph's for 30 years, and they turned out to be important years for the school. In 1971, a made-for-TV movie was produced by Columbia Pictures telling the story of the life and eventual passing of former Bears running back Brian Piccolo. The movie was titled *Brian's Song,* and it remains to this day one of the most popular and powerful movies ever made. St. Joseph's College was used for many of the training scenes.

In 1975, the Bears "transferred" to another school. They set up a permanent training camp home at Lake Forest College in Lake Forest, a small suburb north of Chicago. In 1978, the Bears built their own building on the south campus of Lake Forest College, called it Halas Hall and operated on campus throughout the year. All team offices were in the building. The contract reached with Lake Forest was for 20 years.

By 1997, the Bears had built their own home in Lake Forest, spending $20 million to construct the structures, which include all ownership and front-office personnel facilities, indoor and outdoor practice fields, and full training facilities for weight lifting and physical maintenance. The indoor facility, known as "The Bubble," is named the Walter Payton Center in honor of the Bears Hall of Fame running back.

In 2013, the Bears announced plans to renovate Halas Hall, to include improved facilities for the staff and the media. There are also going to be facilities that allow groups of up to 40 to watch Bears practice outdoors.

In 1984, the Bears again wanted to get out of town for summer training, and they signed a contract to work out at the University of Wisconsin-Platteville, 200 miles northwest of Lake Forest.

Platteville was always an experience for players, media, and fans. The Bears would stay on campus for five weeks at a time, move in with all of their necessities like TVs, video games, and small refrigerators, and the team would take over the small college town. The nightlife in Platteville certainly picked up on the times when the team was allowed to leave campus.

The Platteville experience was also known for what occurred on the last day of training camp. The Bears players would high-tail it out of Platteville in a hurry to get back to big-city civilization, and the race to get home was an event, sometimes including traffic stops when the players were in too much of a hurry to get home.

In 2001, the Bears left Platteville and moved their summer training camp to Olivet Nazarene University, a small school south of the city of Chicago. In 2012, Olivet Nazarene estimated more than 100,000 fans visited the campus during the Bears training camp that summer.

Through the Platteville and Bourbonnais years, visiting Bears summer training camp was one of the best opportunities fans have to see how the Bears operate, how they practice, how they prepare for the upcoming season. But in 2020, the Bears announced they would conduct their summer training camp at their permanent facility in Lake Forest. Plans called for some fan attendance at practices but were not likely to be as inviting as the college campus experiences.

23 Mike Ditka (the Player)

In the history of professional sports, rarely, if ever, has a player or coach so epitomized the reputation of the team for which he worked than Mike Ditka did for the Chicago Bears. That he represented the Bears as both player *and* coach makes his relationship with the team extraordinary.

Hard-nosed, flamboyant, noisy, critical, combative, and competitive, Ditka embodied the spirit of the Chicago Bears, who for the entire 20th century were known for being tougher than their opponents. Ditka was tough all right, whether he was in the game or calling it from the sidelines.

Born and raised in the iron-rich hills of Pennsylvania, Ditka played college football at the University of Pittsburgh. As a tight end for the Panthers, Ditka starred for three years and was an All-American tight end. To this day, he is considered one of the best college tight ends ever, and is a member of the College Football Hall of Fame.

Ditka was drafted fifth overall by the Bears in 1961. In his rookie season, wearing jersey No. 89, he had 56 catches, redefining the position of tight end as an offensive threat rather than just as a blocking position. He was named Rookie of the Year in 1961. Ditka was a member of the Bears' 1963 championship team, which was the most regaled Bears team in franchise history until the 1985 Super Bowl–winning team, which Ditka coached. From his 56 catches in 1961, he caught 58 in 1962, 59 in 1963, and 75 in 1964.

When he was coming out of college, several other NFL teams (Washington, Pittsburgh, and San Francisco) had interest in Ditka, but only as a linebacker. Ditka said Halas was the one who saw him as a new form of offensive player from the tight end position, where he would be covered not by a defensive back but by a linebacker that Ditka could outrun or outmaneuver.

"A lot of people never threw to the tight end," former Bears quarterback Bill Wade said. "I thought it was a pretty good play to call."

On October 13, 1963, Ditka caught nine passes for 110 yards and scored four times (three on passes from Wade) against the Los Angeles Rams as the Bears won the game 52–14. In the low-scoring 1963 Championship Game against the New York Giants, Ditka caught three passes for 38 yards while winning his first NFL title.

Ditka played for the Bears through the 1966 season. If any player seemed perfect to play his entire career with the Bears, it was Ditka. But he argued frequently with Halas over money (as did everybody, it seems), and in 1967 he was traded to the Philadelphia Eagles. He played for the Eagles for two years, then went on to play four seasons with the Dallas Cowboys. In 1972, Ditka caught a touchdown pass for the Cowboys in Super Bowl VI, becoming a two-time NFL champion.

Ditka retired as a player in 1972. He joined the Cowboys staff as an assistant coach in charge of tight ends. In 1982 he became head coach of the Bears. In 1988, he became the first tight end enshrined in the Pro Football Hall of Fame.

On May 24, 2013, the Bears announced plans to retire Ditka's No. 89 jersey, and the ceremony occurred on December 9, 2013, at halftime of a Monday night game at Soldier Field against the Cowboys. Ditka was the 14th player to have his jersey number retired by the Bears.

In 2019, the NFL announced its top 100 players in the league's 100-year history and Ditka made the team as one of five tight ends.

24 Buddy Ryan

Buddy Ryan was the Bears' defensive coordinator from 1978 to 1985, and was entrenched in his position when the Bears switched head coaches, firing Neill Armstrong and replacing him with Mike Ditka. Bears owner George Halas made the unusual decision to force Ryan upon Ditka rather than allowing the new coach to select his own defensive coordinator. That decision led to one of the most successful yet dysfunctional coaching relationships ever.

After serving as an assistant coach at several universities, Ryan got his first professional job with the New York Jets in 1968. He was the team's defensive line coach for eight years, and won his first Super Bowl ring for the Jets' famous upset victory over the Baltimore Colts in Super Bowl III.

In 1976, he became the defensive line coach for the Minnesota Vikings, and for two years directed the Purple People Eaters, the defense that included Hall of Fame players like Alan Page and Carl Eller. The Vikings lost in Super Bowl XI with Ryan on the staff.

In 1978, Ryan got his job as defensive coordinator for the Bears, at a time when Neill Armstrong was a rookie head coach of the team. In 1982, the Bears fired Armstrong, and despite the defensive players begging the team to give Ryan the head job, instead the Bears hired former tight end and then Dallas Cowboys assistant coach Mike Ditka to serve as head coach. Ryan was retained as defensive coordinator.

Ryan's defensive belief was that the key to stopping the opponent was stopping the quarterback. With the Jets, he began his process of developing blitz packages that would put pressure on the opposing team's QB. With Minnesota, he had a defensive line that could be disruptive.

Buddy Ryan is carried off the field by his defense after the Bears crushed the Patriots by a score of 46–10 in Super Bowl XX.

With the Bears, he eventually had both. He developed the 46 defense, which had nothing to do with the number "46" but instead meant that seven players would be in the "box," or close to the line of scrimmage, on every snap, with the possibility of any player coming hard at the quarterback on any play. It was dependent on the belief that the four defensive backs could handle any passing attack, especially if the QB was rushed to get rid of the ball by the blitz package.

Ryan was fiercely protective of his defensive players, and squabbled whenever Ditka tried to have an influence on that side of the game plan.

When the Bears won the Super Bowl, the offensive players carried Ditka off the field at the New Orleans Superdome while the defensive players carried Ryan off. That was seen as a slap in the face of Ditka, but the two had feuded so severely through their years together that it was not a surprise.

It was, however, the end of the relationship, as Ryan was hired in 1986 to become head coach of the Philadelphia Eagles, his first head coaching job. He stayed with them for five seasons, then was the head coach of the Arizona Cardinals for two seasons in 1994 and 1995.

25 Ryan vs. Ditka

The Chicago Bears have had a number of great rivalries over the years—the Chicago Cardinals, the Packers, the Vikings, the Lions, and on and on. But the Bears had an internal rivalry during their greatest Super Bowl–era years that sometimes overshadowed the on-the-field combativeness.

When Mike Ditka was named coach of the Bears in 1982, he was not allowed to name his own defensive coordinator. George Halas, the owner of the Bears, liked Buddy Ryan, whom he had brought in from Minnesota four years earlier. So Ditka, whose football knowledge leaned toward the offensive side of the ball anyway, already had a defensive plan in place for his first coaching tenure.

Ryan, meanwhile, was displeased that Halas had not named him head coach of the team. Such emotional ingredients were set in place that it would have been difficult for Ditka and Ryan to ever get along.

Ryan also felt that Ditka had skipped a step on his progression to head coach. In Ryan's eyes, the correct order of coaching ascension was to be a position coach, then a coordinator, then a head coach. Ditka had come over from being a tight ends coach in Dallas to his first job as a head coach, overstepping Ryan. Such was the atmosphere of the relationship between the two stubborn men.

Still, considering the success of the team, there should have been enough praise to go around. Unfortunately, neither man was happy with the arrangement or the way the accolades were shared.

The defense Ryan had installed prior to Ditka's arrival, which became known as the 46 defense, was revolutionary and extraordinarily successful, to the point that the 1985 Bears who employed the 46 are still considered one of the top three defenses in the history of the NFL.

But the success of the defense, and the attention that was paid to it, created a problem of egos and shared attention between head coach and defensive coordinator. While the Bears were completing their march through the NFL on the way to the Super Bowl in 1986, Ditka and Ryan became embattled over who should receive the lion's share of the credit for the team.

Ditka, a prideful man with a strong backbone (metaphorically speaking), expected the success of the team to be chalked up on his side of the coaching ledger. And it was. Ditka was Coach of the Year in 1985 (an award he received again in 1988) and eventually became the second most important member of the Bears' historical hierarchy behind George Halas.

But the defense in 1985 was almost always the story, despite the presence of Walter Payton on the offensive side of the ball. And when questions were asked or accolades doled out for the defense, Ryan was the coaching recipient more times than not.

In 1985, Ditka pulled his weight and got the Bears to select William Perry out of Clemson in the first round. Ryan thought it was a wasted pick, because of Perry's weight. Eventually, Perry turned out to be a key part of the defense with his line play, and also contributed on the offensive side of the ball as an impossible-to-stop running back.

While Ryan was defensive coordinator, Ditka had almost no contact with the defensive players. That's why, when Ditka got involved in coaching the defense in one of the most famous regular season games in Bears history, Ryan took "offense" to his meddling.

The Bears were 15–1 in their Super Bowl year, and the loss came at Miami on a Monday night game against the Dolphins. Ditka reportedly told Ryan to assign a defensive back to Miami wide receiver Nat Moore, who was covered by linebacker Wilber Marshall in the first half. Ryan refused to agree to employ Ditka's coaching maneuver, and Ditka allegedly challenged Ryan to a fight, suggesting they "go right out back and get it on." It is uncertain whether any physical contact took place. The Bears lost the game 38–24, the only blemish on what is considered one of the best overall seasons for any team ever in the NFL.

Still, the Bears kept winning, and their victory over New England by a score of 46–10 was one of the most dominant outcomes in the championship game since the Bears beat the Washington Redskins 73–0 in the 1940 title contest. But, in victory, the Bears players threw gasoline on the Ditka-Ryan rivalry by showing respect not only for their head coach but also for their defensive coordinator.

As Ditka was being carried off the field primarily by offensive players, the defensive squad picked up Ryan and carried him off the field as well. There were two generals being celebrated in victory. In almost every scenario, that's one too many leaders.

The night before the Super Bowl, Ryan announced he was leaving the Bears to coach the Philadelphia Eagles. The Bears and Eagles were scheduled to meet in the 1986 season, setting up the first of four meetings between teams coached by Ditka and Ryan.

The Bears won all four of those games, including a playoff game at Soldier Field on New Year's Eve 1988.

In November of 2010, at a celebration of the Super Bowl–winning team 25 years later, Ditka and Ryan finally settled their differences, in a way. Behind closed doors, prior to the celebration dinner and event, the two men, ages 71 and 79 by that time, hugged. And thus ended one of the great rivalries in Bears history.

26 Wrigley Field

After moving the team from Decatur, Illinois, to Chicago in 1921, George Halas needed to find a home field for the team. At the time, the largest outdoor facility in the Chicago area was Cubs Park, the structure currently known as Wrigley Field, which was the Cubs' baseball home. The Bears moved in for the 1921 season, and stayed until 1970, when they finally acquiesced to pressure from the NFL and moved into the stadium on the Lake Michigan waterfront, Soldier Field.

In 1926, Cubs Park had its name changed to Wrigley Field in honor of the team's owner, William Wrigley.

An NFL field today is 120 yards long (including 10 yards at each end zone) and 531/3 yards wide. Wrigley Field has always been one of the smaller baseball stadiums in the United States, although Northwestern University did host a game there in 2010 and has a contract for more football games in the future. But football in Wrigley Field is a tight squeeze, and it got tighter as the game got more popular.

For the Bears, the football field inside Wrigley Field was set up to run from the first-base foul line due north into left field.

Staley Field

The first home of the Chicago Bears was Wrigley Field. The first home of the Decatur Staleys was Staley Field.

The team that became the Chicago Bears was originally owned and operated by the A.E. Staley Manufacturing Company, which produced starch from corn. Since the Staley company owned the team and its manufacturing plant was in the central Illinois town of Decatur, they were unofficially referred to throughout history as the Decatur Staleys.

The team played one year in Decatur with George Halas as a player and coach. The Staleys played on the company's athletic field, known as Staley Field, which was situated behind the plant. According to Baseball-Reference.com, Staley Field was used for a minor league baseball team before football was played there.

For anyone in or near Decatur, the specifications of the field are East Eldorado, Cinder Drive, 22nd Street, and North 7th Street.

Staley Manufacturing remains a vital part of the Decatur community, and remains situated at 2200 East Eldorado Street.

Conditions were far from ideal, mostly because the football field barely fit into the confines of the Friendly Confines. Neither end zone was sufficiently large. The end zone near the first-base line ran into the visiting team dugout, while the end zone in left field was short and ended at Wrigley Field's brick walls. Eventually, padding was placed upon those walls to prevent players from injuring themselves as they ran headlong into the wall. In 1937, Cubs owner Bill Veeck planted ivy to grow on the outfield walls, and that remains one of the quaint and unique features of the ballpark.

In what today is considered an apocryphal story, Bears running back Bronko Nagurski is said to have run into an outfield wall at Wrigley after scoring a touchdown by plowing through or around numerous defenders. Upon returning to the huddle, Nagurski reportedly said, "That last guy hit me awfully hard."

In 1921, the seating capacity for Cubs Park was just 15,000, but that number grew as more stands were built for baseball. After a few years, the Bears built portable bleacher seats for the football season that increased the capacity for football to around 47,000.

In 1933, when the NFL started having playoffs, the Bears won the first title with a 23–21 win over the New York Giants at Wrigley Field. They lost the 1937 title to the Washington Redskins at Wrigley 28–21, beat the Giants again for the 1941 title 37–9, and won the title again at home in 1943 against the Redskins.

In 1963, Wrigley Field saw its last NFL Championship Game, when the Bears of Bill George and Doug Atkins once again topped the New York Giants, this time 14–10. The NFL had asked the Bears to play the game at Soldier Field because it had lights and a higher seating capacity, but Bears owner George Halas refused.

On December 13, 1970, the Bears played their last game at Wrigley Field in a 35–17 win over the hated rival Green Bay Packers.

After a 40-year absence, football came back to Wrigley Field on November 20, 2010, when the Northwestern Wildcats hosted the University of Illinois Illini in a game at the historic ballpark. Due to changes that had occurred to the seating areas and field over the previous 40 years, the teams played with only one useable end zone, so that the team on offense would always be playing toward the western end zone, where the home team dugout is.

In February of 2013, Northwestern and the Chicago Cubs signed a long-term deal for Wrigley to host more football games, as well as collegiate lacrosse, soccer, and, of course, baseball games.

27 Jim McMahon

Quarterback is the most important position on a football team, and is arguably the most important position in any team sport. But the Bears had the hardest time getting that position right for decades.

After Sid Luckman ended his illustrious career as the Bears starting QB in 1948, the franchise struggled to find a long-term answer at that position. Johnny Lujack followed Luckman for three seasons, George Blanda played the position for two years in the middle of his Hall of Fame career, and Billy Wade led the team to the 1963 championship in his four years at the spot. But once Wade left the club in 1965, the team went through numerous quarterbacks without a great deal of success.

Bobby Douglass, a lefty, was notable for his ability to run out of the quarterback position. Bob Avellini had the look of a quarterback and held the spot for three years. Then, in 1982, the Bears brought former tight end Mike Ditka in to coach the team, and Ditka convinced the Bears to draft Jim McMahon out of Brigham Young University.

McMahon, the fifth pick in the 1982 NFL Draft, came to the Bears with a reputation as a gunslinger quarterback, and held numerous Brigham Young and NCAA records from his two-plus years as quarterback of the Cougars. When he left Brigham Young as an ungraduated senior, he owned dozens of NCAA passing records. He finished third in balloting for the 1981 Heisman Trophy.

McMahon came to the Bears with a reputation as a fearless leader on the football field. The conclusion of his 1980 season was in the Holiday Bowl, when the Cougars played Southern

Methodist University. The Mustangs built a 45–25 lead with four minutes remaining in a wild contest. But McMahon led the Cougars back with three touchdowns, including the game-tying 41-yard heave to Clay Brown as time expired. The Cougars needed the extra point to win the game, which they did, 46–45. The game was called "The Miracle Bowl," and McMahon had boosted his draft status considerably.

McMahon joined a Bears team that was thirsty for victory. His job was to present a different weapon so that defenses could not hone in on Walter Payton, who was seven years into his illustrious career without a single Super Bowl appearance to his name.

Once the city of Chicago got to know McMahon, the question that came up time and again was "Why was he playing football at Brigham Young?" His behavior was outlandish from the start, and grew to legendary status once the Bears won the Super Bowl.

He also developed a reputation for getting hurt, due to his rough-and-tumble approach to the game, as well as a reputation for playing thorough pain. He had to be talked off the field in a playoff game in 1984 after suffering bruised ribs and a lacerated kidney.

Almost all photos of McMahon show him wearing sunglasses. At the age of six, he accidentally stabbed himself in the eye with a fork. It did not affect his vision, but it did make him very sensitive to light. He was extremely uncomfortable whenever he was without shading over his eyes.

The 1985 NFL season was magical for the Bears, as they marched to the Super Bowl and crushed the New England Patriots in the game itself. But the voyage to the Super Bowl was as memorable as the game itself, and McMahon played a role in the spectacular manner in which the Bears won.

Brazened by the team's success, McMahon went out in the NFC divisional playoff game against the New York Giants by wearing a headband with the Adidas logo on it. The NFL had contracts with a different equipment supplier, and McMahon was fined by the commissioner's office for the infraction. When the Bears played the Los Angeles Rams in the NFC title game, McMahon came out with a headband that had the hand-scrawled name "Rozelle" on it, a reference to NFL commissioner Pete Rozelle.

The 1985 Bears made news and established themselves as the cockiest football team ever when they made a video called "The Super Bowl Shuffle," which they took part in *before they qualified to play in the Super Bowl.* McMahon had a role in the video, calling himself "the punky QB." The video was made public after the Bears won the NFC Championship Game.

During Super Bowl week in New Orleans, McMahon was the target of the media looking for stories to sell newspapers. He was videoed dropping his pants and pointing his rear end in the direction of a TV station helicopter flying over their practice field.

McMahon represented himself well in the Super Bowl. He completed 12 of 20 passes for 256 yards. He scored twice, on runs of two and one yards, becoming the first quarterback ever to score two rushing touchdowns in a Super Bowl.

The post–Super Bowl years were not kind to McMahon. He stayed with the Bears through the 1988 season, but injuries kept taking him out of the lineup. He played just six games in 1986, seven in 1987 and nine in 1988.

On November 23, 1986, the Bears were playing the Green Bay Packers at Soldier Field. After a pass attempt by McMahon, Packers defensive end Charles Martin picked McMahon up off the ground and slammed him to the turf, further injuring McMahon's already hampered shoulder. McMahon was out for the rest of the season, and suffered shoulder problems the rest of his career. Martin was suspended for two games.

In seven seasons for the Bears, McMahon completed 57.8 percent of his passes and had 67 touchdowns with 56 interceptions. He also had 15 rushing touchdowns and caught three passes, scoring twice.

In all, McMahon played for six teams after his Bears stint, ending his career with the Green Bay Packers. He never managed to play more than 12 games in a season during those years.

28 How the Bears Got Their Name

The Chicago Bears remain one of the most recognizable professional sports brands in American culture. Few sports names seem so perfectly descriptive of the team it represents.

Chicago is known for its brutal winters. It is not uncommon for someone to suggest that the upcoming winter is going to be "a bear." When teams come into Chicago on cold November or December days, they are told they are about to face Bear Weather. Bears (the animals) are protected against conditions with a layer of fur, and are tough in the elements. As names go, George Halas got it correct.

The Chicago Bears started as the Decatur Staleys, named after the company that sponsored the pro team in 1919, the A.E. Staley Food Starch Company of Decatur, Illinois. When Mr. Staley wanted to sell the team in 1921, he turned to George Halas, who was his coach and star player, and Halas bought the team and moved it to Chicago. Halas was contractually obligated to keep the "Staley" name for one year in Chicago.

Upon completion of the first and only season as the Chicago Staleys, when the team won the American Professional Football League title, Halas was looking for a new name. The Staleys had played their inaugural season at Cubs Park, which would eventually be renamed Wrigley Field, the home of baseball's Chicago Cubs. In honor of Cubs owner Bill Veeck, who had agreed to

The Logo

The Chicago Bears' logo is a wishbone lying on its side. It is an orange "C" bordered by a thin stripe of white, which is bordered by a thin stripe of blue.

While that sounds simple, it is a more complicated version of the original "C" which was just a white wishbone "C" surrounded by a stripe of black.

The Bears did have a different logo but did not employ one until the 1940s, when George Halas had someone draw up a running bear with a football in its grasp. Eventually, it was changed to a bear standing on top of a football. In 1962, the "C" became the team's top visual representation, and was needed because the league was requiring logos on helmets. The "C" worked better than the balancing bear.

let the football team use the baseball facility for its home games, Halas wanted to come up with a name that would be associated with the Cubs.

Cubs are the offspring of Bears. Football is a meaner and tougher game than baseball. Therefore, it was pretty simple for Halas to come up with the name "Chicago Bears" for his APFL team.

The Bears organization respects its role as one of the founding members of the NFL, and that respect extends to its uniform and logos. The Bears have made very few changes to either of its standard representations, even as other teams have tried to go with outlandish costumes and marketing-focused signage.

The Bears' current logo is a standard letter "C" that is pinched off in the middle to make it look like a sideways wishbone. That logo has represented the team since 1962. Prior to that, the Bears' logo was the depiction of a bear (the animal) standing on top of a football. In some retro hat designs, that logo can be seen today.

The "C" is printed in a silhouette form, and today is a blue-bordered "C" with an orange band of color inside.

The blue and orange colors are a tribute from Halas to his college, the University of Illinois, which also sports blue and orange as its colors.

Over the years, the Bears have seen all possible combinations of blue, white, and orange jerseys and pants. They played one game in the 1930s in all orange, a look they did not return to until the 2000s, when other teams were experimenting with loud or wild uniform designs. Today the standard Bears uniform is a blue jersey with white pants at home and a white jersey with blue pants on the road. The blue-on-blue combination occasionally attempted by the Bears was striking, although the Bears lost their first two games in that uniform combination. For the 2008 season, the Bears wore all-white uniforms.

For one game in 1994, the NFL asked teams to wear throwback uniforms as a way to honor the league's 75th anniversary. The Bears were the one team that could "throw" way back, and they donned the first uniform for the team, which was a blue jersey with brown stripes and brown pants. As a slight nod to modern times, the stripes that were vertical on the 1921 uniform were the same in 1994 with the exception of a V-shaped stripe at the neck of the jersey.

In 2003, the Bears made another concession to modern times and created a mascot that could parade on the sidelines. It was a happy looking bear named Staley to honor the team's first owner. Staley resembled his good friend from the near west side, the original Benny the Bull for the Chicago Bulls.

29 Retired Numbers

A long-standing tradition in team sports is for a team to honor its greatest players by "retiring" their jersey numbers, never to be worn by another player. But when a team has a long history, and has players of great historic note every decade, that team can get in trouble with its jersey numbers.

So it came to pass that the NFL asked the Chicago Bears to stop retiring jersey numbers, simply so the team could field a squad with one- or two-digit numbers and have enough to supply the full squad.

The Bears lead the NFL in retired jersey numbers with 14. Here is a quick rundown of the numbers, in numerical order, that are never to be worn again by a Chicago Bear:

No. 3—For Bronko Nagurski, the sturdy two-way player who played for the Bears from 1930 to 1937 and then came out of retirement to play again in 1943 and help the Bears claim a title.

No. 5—For George McAfee, a running back who played for the Bears in 1940 and '41, went off to serve in the Navy from 1942 to 1945, then returned to play for the Bears from 1945 to 1950.

No. 7—For George Halas, for his years as a player, coach, and team owner.

No. 28—For Willie Galimore, a running back who played for the Bears from 1957 to 1963. His number was retired after he was killed in an automobile accident in the summer of 1964.

No. 34—For Walter Payton, the running back who played for the Bears from 1975 to 1987 and retired as one of the greatest running backs in NFL history.

No. 40—For Gale Sayers, the Kansas star who was a running back for the Bears for only seven seasons before injuries took their toll.

No. 41—For Brian Piccolo, the running back who played for four years for the Bears along with Sayers from 1966 to 1969 before dying from leukemia. The story of his time with the Bears was told in the made-for-TV movie *Brian's Song*.

No. 42—For Sid Luckman, the best quarterback in Bears history, who played for the team from 1939 to 1950 and won four championships.

No. 51—For Dick Butkus, the Chicago-born linebacker who played college ball at the University of Illinois before becoming a middle linebacker for the Bears from 1965 to 1973.

No. 56—For Bill Hewitt, who played defensive end for the Bears from 1932 to 1936.

No. 61—For Bill George, the middle linebacker who played for the Bears from 1952 to 1965.

No. 66—For Clyde "Bulldog" Turner, who played center and linebacker for the Bears from 1940 to 1952.

No. 77—For Red Grange, the University of Illinois running back who had to be convinced to play professional football in 1925 then came back and played for the team from 1929 to 1934.

No. 89—For Mike Ditka, the first star two-way tight end (blocking and receiving) in NFL history, and later the coach of the 1985 Super Bowl champion team.

There is a great deal of argument among Bears fans about the fact that only one player from the 1985 Super Bowl team—Payton—has had his jersey number retired, and he was on the offensive side of the ball, when the defense was the dominant side of the team. Defensive tackle Dan Hampton (No. 99), linebacker Mike Singletary (No. 50), and defensive end Richard Dent (No. 95), who are all in the Pro Football Hall of Fame, are most often suggested as possible candidates. But with 14 numbers retired, taking away another possible jersey number for future players would handcuff the team in spring and summer training because they would have only 86 possible jersey numbers available from 0 to 100.

30 Halas and Lombardi

Vince Lombardi became coach of the Green Bay Packers in 1959. At that point, George Halas had been coaching for almost 40 years, and had literally seen everything that made the NFL the successful sports league that it was.

But Lombardi came in with a football philosophy that succeeded, and won five titles in nine seasons, including the first two Super Bowls. He was a thorn in Halas' side, which is why the rivalry and begrudging friendship between Halas and Lombardi is considered the greatest such relationship in NFL history.

Let's start with Halas, since he got involved in professional football all the way back in 1920, when he was hired to play for and coach the Decatur Staleys. One year later, he was owner of the Chicago Staleys, turned them into the Chicago Bears, then attended the meeting in Ohio when the NFL was born.

Prior to Lombardi's entry into the NFL, Halas had won seven NFL titles. He had reinvented offensive football with the installation of the T-formation. He'd been witness to the invention of the middle linebacker on the defensive side of the ball. He was known as "Papa Bear" not only because he created the Bears, but was also in some ways the father of professional football.

Halas already had a relationship with a Green Bay coach. From 1919 to 1949, Curly Lambeau had been in charge of the

Packers both on the field and in the front office. The rivalry between the Bears and Packers became heated initially because Lambeau and Halas would do whatever they could to gain an edge over the other.

In 1956, Halas made an unusual trek to Green Bay to speak to city leaders and encourage them to build a new stadium for the Packers, who were in danger of leaving the community for a larger city. Thanks to Halas' pleas and negotiations, the city approved the funds necessary to build what became Lambeau Field. Without Halas' involvement, there might not have been a Packers team for Lombardi to coach.

Lombardi was just six years old when Halas signed his first contract with the Staleys. He was first a high school coach before becoming a college assistant and eventually an assistant with the New York Giants before the Packers hired him to be their head coach in 1959.

The Bears-Packers rivalry was already red hot when Lombardi arrived. From 1933, when the NFL first starting having official championship games, until 1958, the Bears and Packers had combined to win eight NFL titles (five for the Bears). There was already a healthy hatred among fans of both teams.

Lombardi arrived to save the Green Bay Packers. The previous season, 1958, the Packers were 1–10–1, and were in financial difficulties due to poor results. Lombardi arrived with some notoriety as the offensive genius behind the success of the New York Giants. He had created a new offensive line scheme that called for linemen to block areas rather than specific defensive players, creating holes for the running back that were pre-designed and not determined by the way the defensive line lined up.

Lombardi improved the Packers enough in his first year to be named Coach of the Year. He got the Packers to the title game in 1960, when they lost to the Philadelphia Eagles, then won the championship in both 1961 and '62.

Meanwhile, the Bears had not won a title since 1946. Halas was not accustomed to any long stretch of non-championships. But in 1960 he knew he was building a contending team. He just had to get past Lombardi's Packers.

Lombardi was very vocal about his respect for Halas, saying that the Bears' leader was the only man he called "Coach." But Lombardi enjoyed needling Halas, calling him occasionally to suggest trades that he knew Halas would turn down, just to get on his nerves.

To no one's surprise, Halas and Lombardi were both named to the NFL's 100-year roster as two of the 10 best coaches in the league's history.

31 Bill George

Seemingly forever, the Chicago Bears have been known for having the best middle linebackers in the game. That tradition started with Bill George, who played for the Bears from 1952 to 1965. History suggests George created the position of middle linebacker during his time with the Bears.

The Chicago Bears drafted George out of Wake Forest University in the second round of the NFL Draft in 1951, though he didn't begin playing for the Bears until 1952. He was drafted to play defensive middle guard, a position that existed when football teams played with what was then considered the standard five-man front (a formation that was used to defend against the run, which was much more prevalent than the forward pass in those days).

In a game in 1954, George adjusted his playing style. After discussing the plan with linebacker George Connor (another Bears

Hall of Famer), George decided rather than run into the opposing team's center at the snap, George would drop back into a coverage area, affecting the ability of the quarterback from the opposing team to pass the ball into the middle of the field. George altered his plan of attack after realizing his initial thrust into the line allowed the quarterback to simply pass the ball over his head and into the empty area behind him.

George never truly stopped appearing on the defensive line. He made the opposition guess whether he was going to charge forward or drop back into coverage. He was so adept at reading the intentions of the other team that he became the on-field coach of the Bears defense, serving as a field general through most of his years with the team.

Today, the defensive guard position has disappeared. Teams either play four men fronts, with two defensive ends and two defensive tackles, or go with a 3-4 alignment, with four linebackers behind two defensive ends and one defensive tackle. Either way, the change was all because of George's decision to back off the line and drop into coverage.

George also had the athletic ability that has come to typify a middle linebacker—the ability to play the entire field when necessary. He could move side to side as well as forward and back, and his range of coverage area was remarkable.

In 14 seasons with the Bears, George had 18 interceptions, and was credited with 17 fumble recoveries. He also played the position of kicker for the Bears in 1954, when he scored a total of 25 points on 13 PATs and four field goals.

George was named to the Pro Bowl eight consecutive years starting in 1954, and was named to the Pro Football Hall of Fame in 1974.

32 Gale Sayers

Considered one of the greatest open-field runners in college and professional football history, Gale Sayers played for the Chicago Bears for just seven seasons before a series of knee injuries took him out of the game. But in his short time in the league, Sayers outperformed everybody else at the time, and set records even though the Bears never made the playoffs in his entire career.

In 1965, the Chicago Bears had the third and fourth picks in the first round of the draft. With the third pick, they selected linebacker Dick Butkus out of the University of Illinois, a local high school star who stayed close to home to play football. With the fourth pick, they selected Gale Sayers, who likewise stayed close to home, playing for the University of Kansas. The two players ended up in both the College and Pro Football Halls of Fame.

Sayers came to the Bears with a reputation from his college days. He made Kansas competitive in the ultracompetitive Big Eight Conference for football, and was a two-time All-American. He was known as "the Kansas Comet," a nickname that set him up as a focal point of defenses in the NFL.

That didn't matter. He became the unanimous choice for NFL Rookie of the Year after scoring 20 touchdowns from scrimmage (14 on the ground, six through the air) as well as one punt return and one kickoff return for a score. He set an NFL record with 2,272 all-purpose yards while gaining 1,374 yards from scrimmage in his first season.

On December 12, 1965, the Bears hosted the San Francisco 49ers, who had beaten the Bears 52–24 in the opening game of the season. That started the Bears on an 0–3 record at the beginning of what became a 9–5 campaign.

Gale Sayers' wife, Linda, looks on as he shakes hands with Papa Bear Halas after signing with the Bears on December 1, 1965.

The second game against San Francisco was the next to last game of the season, and it was played on a rain-soaked surface at Wrigley Field. But that didn't seem to matter to Sayers, who had touchdown runs of 21 yards, seven yards, 50 yards, and one yard, plus his first touchdown, an 80-yard reception from quarterback Rudy Bukich. In the fourth quarter, with the Bears ahead 47–20, Sayers scored on an 85-yard punt return, and that ended his six-touchdown day.

That tied the NFL record held by Chicago Cardinals running back Ernie Nevers and Cleveland Browns running back Dub Jones. There was still time left on the clock, but coach George Halas decided Sayers had done enough. The Bears got another rushing touchdown later in the game, and had Sayers been allowed to attempt that one, he could have had the record himself.

Sayers led the league in rushing in his second season, and raised his NFL record for all-purpose yards to 2,440. His rushing numbers were down because the Bears had another decent running back named Brian Piccolo playing in the fullback position. In 1967, Sayers scored three touchdowns on kickoffs and one on a punt return.

Late in the 1968 season, Sayers suffered the first of several injuries, tearing ligaments in his right knee. He came back in the 1969 season and led the league in rushing yet again, but his numbers were down, his yards-per-carry average was down, and he was clearly not the same runner as before the first injury.

In the 1970 season, Sayers suffered an injury to his left knee, which effectively ended his career. He played in two games in 1970 and two more in 1971, but did not score again, and had only 36 carries in those four games total.

Because he retired after the 1971 season at the age of 29, and because he was a first-ballot Hall of Famer, he became the youngest player ever to enter the Pro Football Hall of Fame at the age of 34. George Halas was Sayers' presenter on his induction day.

During his rehabilitation from his two knee injuries, his constant companion and continual pain in the neck was teammate Brian Piccolo, the fullback who was getting Sayers' carries while he was hurt. Sayers and Piccolo were so close, they became the first roommates in NFL history from different races—Sayers an African American and Piccolo a Caucasian.

Piccolo's kindness to Sayers was paid back in 1969 when Piccolo was diagnosed with testicular cancer. Piccolo died in June of 1970 at the age of 26, and Sayers was with him throughout his ordeal, as Piccolo was for Sayers.

The friendship between Sayers and Piccolo was the subject of one of the best made-for-TV movies ever, titled *Brian's Song,* a tearjerker about men who became friends despite a difference in skin color, upbringing, and talent level.

Following his premature retirement, Sayers remained an icon in Chicago for the next 15 years, until Walter Payton came along.

In 2019, the NFL named the top 100 players in the league's first 100 years, and despite playing only seven seasons, Sayers made the cut, one of eight Bears players selected to that list.

33 Johnny Lujack

In 1946, the Chicago Bears drafted a quarterback out of the University of Notre Dame named Johnny Lujack. What made that pick unusual was that he had two years remaining with the Irish.

There was no greater star in college football than Johnny Lujack. Although his career at Notre Dame was interrupted by a two-year stint in the Navy during World War II, Lujack won three national championships as the starting quarterback for the Irish. He played basketball, baseball and ran track as well. He won the 1947 Heisman Trophy following an undefeated season. He appeared on the cover of magazines that weren't even sports related. He was a star.

In 1948, his first year with the Bears, he played quarterback behind Sid Luckman, who was a hero in Chicago for leading the Bears to the four championships, and today is still considered the best Bears quarterback ever. But Lujack, in spot quarterback duty, had numbers similar to Luckman's, including a nearly identical completion rate, a better yards-per-catch rate, a better touchdown percentage, a better interception percentage, and (using a stat which didn't exist back then) a much better quarterback rating.

In 1949, Lujack was the starter, and he threw 23 touchdown passes in 12 games, and averaged 222 yards per game. Luckman threw just 50 passes that year, and George Blanda, who was brought on board for kicking duties, had just 21 pass attempts.

The final game of the 1949 season was against the Chicago Cardinals, and the Bears won 52–21. Lujack threw for six touchdowns and 468 yards, which was an NFL record. The next season, Lujack set the NFL record for most rushing touchdowns by a quarterback, reaching the end zone 11 times by foot. Unfortunately, his passing numbers were horrible, with 21 interceptions and only four touchdowns that season.

Lujack played just four seasons for the Bears before returning to Notre Dame to serve as an assistant coach. He extended his football life by becoming a broadcaster, working for CBS on the NFL and for both CBS and ABC for college football telecasts.

So why did Lujack play only four seasons for the Bears, leaving the team in 1951 at the age of 26? It was for the same reason Mike Ditka did not end his playing career with the Bears: he argued with George Halas over money.

Lujack did not want to play for the Bears for the $20,000 he was making, and after repeated attempts to get Halas to pay him more, Lujack just decided to stop playing. The Bears announced that he was retiring due to injury, but the truth was different. In fact, the Bears tried to trade Lujack, but the demands made to the Chicago Cardinals and Los Angeles Rams at the time were so outrageous no deal was done. In the 1950s, players were bound to the team that owned their NFL rights unless traded or released, and the Bears did neither for Lujack, who moved on to start an automobile business.

34 Chicago Cardinals

If someone asked you "Which team is the Bears' most hated rival?" you would be correct to say "The Green Bay Packers." But if someone asked you "Who was the Bears' first hated rival?" the answer would be the Chicago Cardinals.

The Chicago Cardinals is a team that had its roots in the city long before there was an NFL, or its predecessor, the American Professional Football Association. But when it came time to form a structured league of professional football in this country, the Cardinals were in the 1920 meeting, along with the Decatur Staleys, who became the Chicago Bears. There were 14 teams in the league that first year, ranging from Buffalo, New York to Rock Island, Illinois. The Cardinals and Bears were in it, but the Green Bay Packers did not join the league until 1921.

From the beginning, the Cardinals and Bears had a thorny relationship on the field. The Cardinals gave the Staleys their only loss in 1920, preventing them from winning the league title. In 1922, the Bears lost three games out of 12, and two of those losses were to the Cardinals, even though the Bears had a better overall record.

The Bears played at Wrigley Field and the Cardinals played at Normal Park on the city's south side. Just as the Chicago Cubs and Chicago White Sox have a rivalry that settles on the north-south boundaries of the city, so did the Bears and Cardinals.

The Cardinals won the 1925 NFL championship, but following that season, they had only two winning seasons in the next 20 years. They then managed four consecutive winning seasons from 1946 to 1949. They won the title in 1947 by beating the Philadelphia Eagles, and they lost to the Eagles in the 1948 game.

Although the Cardinals franchise still exists, making Glendale, Arizona, its home, the Cardinals have not won an NFL title since 1947.

The team was originally owned by a Chicago man named Chris O'Brien. He sold the team in 1929 to another man, who sold it in 1932 to Charles Bidwell, who at the time was a vice president of the Bears. To this day, the Bidwell family still owns the Cardinals, in much the same way the Halas family continues to own the Bears. The difference between the two franchises is that the Cardinals moved from Chicago to St. Louis and then to Arizona, while the Bears stayed put.

The Cardinals suffered on the field with very few winning seasons through the years in Chicago, and as a result, the Bears were much more popular with the fans. In 1960, under the weight of significant financial difficulties, the Cardinals were allowed by the NFL to move the franchise to St. Louis, Missouri. In 1987, the Cardinals moved again to the Phoenix area to become the Arizona Cardinals.

At the end of the 2012 NFL season, the Bears and Cardinals had played 91 times since 1920, and the Bears had a 58–27–6 record against them. The only teams the Bears have more victories against are the Detroit Lions and the Green Bay Packers.

35 William "the Refrigerator" Perry

It is fair to say that, for a little while at least, William Perry was as big as life.

He was always big, but Perry's weight and his surprising athleticism made him noticeable in his too-short NFL career.

In 1985, the Chicago Bears selected Perry, a one-time All-American out of Clemson, with the 22nd pick in the NFL Draft. He was listed as a defensive lineman, and that's where he played most of his downs with the Chicago Bears. But on a couple of occasions, he played on the offensive side of the ball, and not as a lineman. But that's a story for another paragraph.

Perry was selected as a result of the wishes of head coach Mike Ditka. And, as most of Ditka's decisions did, the move infuriated defensive coordinator Buddy Ryan, with whom Ditka had a very difficult relationship. Ryan called it a "wasted draft pick" publicly, which indicates just how open the gap between Ditka and Ryan was.

Ryan criticized the pick because of Perry's size, which had earned him the nickname "the Refrigerator," a name that eventually was cut down to "the Fridge." On draft day, Perry was listed at 335 pounds, on a 6'2" frame, and Ryan felt Perry's weight would prevent him from being an effective part of his 46 defense, which stressed placing pressure on the opposing quarterback. Ryan played Perry sparingly in the first part of the 1985 season.

Ryan did not seem to care that Perry was an accomplished athlete outside of football. He was surprisingly fast, at least in terms of foot speed, for a player his weight. He could dunk a basketball. He was far more athletic than Ryan was willing to accept.

Because he was the Bears' first-round draft pick that year, and because Ryan was holding him back in terms of playing time on the defensive side of the ball, Ditka decided to put Perry's size and athleticism to good use on the offensive side of the ball.

Late in the 1984 season, prior to Perry's arrival with the Bears, legendary San Francisco coach Bill Walsh used a defensive lineman named Guy McIntyre to serve as a blocking back and running back in a game against the Bears. Ditka didn't like it, because he felt it was showing up his team, but he took note.

So, in a 1985 rematch with the 49ers, Ditka took advantage of Perry's size and used him as a blocking back for Walter Payton. The following week, the Bears played a Monday night game against Green Bay and Perry was again used as a blocking back for Payton. Perry also scored a touchdown from one yard out, and his star shone brightly.

Perry eventually worked his way into the starting lineup on the defensive side of the ball in his rookie season, getting nine starts, and he earned five sacks. He also had five rushes for seven yards and two touchdowns. He also caught a pass for a four-yard touchdown, as Ditka seemed to enjoy teasing the staid NFL with his massive superstar.

The Bears reached the Super Bowl that season, and won it with a convincing 46–10 victory over the New England Patriots. But it was in that game that Ditka's use of Perry on the offensive side of the ball had a negative impact on history.

In the third quarter, with the Bears ahead 37–3, Ditka called for a fullback dive from the 1-yard line, and Perry scored. It was a remarkable call, yet another use for Perry as a kind of effective circus act, but when the game was over, Perry had a Super Bowl touchdown and longtime superstar running back Walter Payton did not. In ensuing years, Ditka said calling on Perry for that touchdown instead of Payton was one of the biggest regrets of his career.

From that point, Perry's celebrity status was beyond the pale. He was everywhere, in commercials, TV shows, and in print. His gap-toothed smile, and his pleasant good ol' country boy demeanor, made him popular not just in Chicago but around the world.

In his time with the Bears, Perry recorded 28.5 sacks. But after Ryan left the team to coach the Philadelphia Eagles, Ditka stopped using Perry for offensive purposes, perhaps because he no longer had to make digs at Ryan. Perry finished his career with the Philadelphia Eagles.

Perry's weight ballooned to as much as 385 pounds by the end of his career, and he suffered severe health problems after retiring in 1995.

36 Devin Hester

Clearly, nobody really knew what Devin Hester was capable of. Otherwise, he would not have been chosen with the 57th overall pick of the 2006 NFL Draft.

The Bears grabbed the University of Miami defensive back in the second round with plans to use him solely as a returner. Although he had experience with the Hurricanes as a receiver and as a cornerback, his role with the 2006 Bears was going to be as a return man.

Hester's first game as a Bear was the season opener against the Green Bay Packers, in which he ripped off a fourth-quarter 84-yard punt return for a touchdown in the Bears' impressive 26–0 win over the hated Packers (and hated Packers quarterback Brett Favre). In the sixth game of the season, when the 5–0 Bears trailed the Arizona Cardinals by the surprise 20–0 halftime score and 23–10 in the fourth quarter of the Monday night contest, Hester returned a punt 83 yards for a touchdown which propelled the Bears to a startling 24–23 win. It was one of the highlights of a season that would end with an appearance in the Super Bowl.

On November 12 of that year, in a game in Giants Stadium in East Rutherford, New Jersey, Hester made his most remarkable play in a most unexpected way. As teams do on long field goals, the Bears had Hester stand under the uprights as Giants kicker Jay Feely attempted a 52-yard field goal. The Bears actually thought

Devin Hester gets past the last man, kicker Adam Vinatieri, on his way to a 92-yard kickoff return for a touchdown on the opening kickoff of Super Bowl XLI.

the Giants were going to fake the field goal and try for a punt that would put the Bears deep into their own territory.

But Feely kicked the ball, and it dropped into Hester's hands eight yards into the end zone; nowhere near long enough for a successful field goal. Hester made one of those decisions that coaches hate, until they turn out to be the right decision. He ran the ball out of the end zone and didn't stop running until he got into the Giants' end zone for a 108-yard touchdown on a missed field goal. That, by the way, is not a category the NFL keeps regular statistics in, because it doesn't happen often.

Oddly enough, the Bears had another 108-yard missed field goal return in 2005 when Nathan Vasher ran the ball back on a ridiculously windy day at Soldier Field.

Against the St. Louis Rams in 2006, Hester returned not one but two kickoffs for touchdowns, one for 94 yards and the other for 96.

The next big moment in Hester's career came on the biggest possible stage. The Bears advanced to the Super Bowl in Hester's first year, playing Peyton Manning and the Indianapolis Colts at Dolphin Stadium in Miami. It was a time of triumphant return for Hester, the former Miami Hurricane. The game started with the Colts kicking off to the Bears, and although teams had taken to trying to avoid Hester with kickoffs near the end of the regular season, no one was going to start the Super Bowl that way. In fact, the Colts special teams players lobbied head coach Tony Dungy to kick off to Hester, promising they would bottle the speedster.

Ask any Bears fan who watched that Super Bowl and they will tell you they knew what was going to happen next. Despite a constant rain that continued the entire game, Hester returned the opening kickoff 92 yards for a touchdown—the first opening-play score in Super Bowl history.

In 2007, the Bears decided that Hester's speed would make him a dangerous wide receiver and started using him on offensive possessions as well. His first year in that role he scored two touchdowns receiving to go with two kickoff returns and four punt returns for touchdowns. By the end of his second season, Hester already held the Bears record for most kicks returned for scores, with a total of 12, a number that included that field goal return.

Hester then went two seasons without a kick return for a score, and some attributed that to the confusion he suffered because of his desire to make more plays as a wide receiver. Prior to the start of the 2008 season, Hester received a new contract that paid him as a wide receiver, with a great number of incentives for receiver performance, and many think that the new contract confused Hester about the best way for him to contribute to the team.

From 2010 through 2012, Hester scored six more touchdowns on kicks, five on punts, and in 2010 he had his best year as a receiver with four touchdown catches. Through his first seven seasons as a Bear, he had 14 touchdowns as a receiver, 17 touchdowns as a kick returner, and one touchdown as a field goal returner.

When the NFL celebrated its 100-year history by naming the best 100 players in league history, Hester was one of two return men named to the squad.

37 1940 NFL Championship Game

On Sunday, November 17, 1940, the Washington Redskins defeated the Chicago Bears 7–3 in a regular season meeting. The loss dropped the Bears to 6–3 for the season, but they won the last two games of the regular campaign to beat out the Green Bay Packers and win the NFL's Western Division, earning a spot in the

NFL Championship Game. The Redskins won the NFL's Eastern Division, setting up a rematch.

The game was played at Washington's home field, Griffith Stadium, on December 8, 1940. Game reports indicate it was a sunny day, but that did not turn out to be the truth for the Redskins. The Bears scored on the game's opening drive, when Bill Osmanski ran 68 yards for a touchdown on the game's second play from scrimmage, and the Bears had a 7–0 lead.

When the game was over, the Bears had won the 1940 NFL championship by the final score of 73–0, not only the largest margin of victory for any NFL Championship Game, but the largest margin of victory for any NFL game ever played.

Ten different members of the Bears scored touchdowns. Three of the Bears' touchdowns came on interception returns. The Bears scored 45 points in the second half, and kept scoring even after Bears coach George Halas replaced all of his starters with backups.

There are few explanations for how this game ended up so lopsided. But there are clues.

For one, Washington owner George Preston Marshall, a long-time rival of George Halas, made disparaging remarks about the Bears after their regular season meeting, at one point being quoted calling them "crybabies."

For the championship game, Halas called on Clark Shaughnessy, a friend who was coaching the Stanford Cardinals college team, and they devised a new running attack that became known as the T-formation (which is so aligned with the Bears' success after that it is referred to in the team's fight song).

There were reports after the game that the Bears scored so many touchdowns that referees were afraid of running out of footballs. Footballs that were used for extra point kicks that went into the stands were not returned in those days, and the Bears had nine balls kicked into the stands that day. Near the end of the game, officials asked Halas to run or pass for the conversion if they scored again just so they could have enough equipment to continue the game.

That game remained one of Halas' favorite football memories for the remainder of his life.

38 "The Super Bowl Shuffle"

The 1985 Chicago Bears were special because they had the most dominant defense in the history of the game. They had the world's most famous 360-pound running back. They had the world's most respected regular-size running back. They had the first "punky" quarterback. They had a loudmouth coach who became a national figure and top-level salesman. They had the most dominant victory in Super Bowl history.

But what made the 1985 Chicago Bears most special is that they filmed a celebration of their Super Bowl status and their unique role in NFL history weeks before they won anything, at a time when no one knew for sure they would win anything.

You have to see this video to understand who the 1985 Bears were, and what kind of swagger they had as a team.

"The Super Bowl Shuffle" is a three-minute video of the Bears performing a rap song that celebrated their team and individual status as NFL superstars. In terms of video quality, it didn't really have much to offer. The players all stood in front of the camera and just sort of moved their hips to the music, repeating the song's refrain.

Some players were featured singers in the video, others "performed" as background musicians, although none of them actually played the instruments they were seen with in the video. Other players participated with vocals on the recording part of the video.

The singers were Richard Dent, Gary Fencik, Steve Fuller, Willie Gault, Jim McMahon, Walter Payton, William Perry, Mike Richardson, Mike Singletary, and Otis Wilson. In all, 24 players from the '85 team participated in "The Super Bowl Shuffle."

Getting Payton involved was considered the key to the success of the song. Although it was created at a time when the Bears were still chasing their title, and there was concern Payton would not want to be involved because of that, the superstar running back decided it would be fun to sing on the record. Payton had a musical background, and had played drums in a rock band in high school.

The refrain was sung several times in the song, in between solo verses from the star players.

"We are the Bears' Shufflin' Crew
Shufflin' on down, doin' it for you.
We're so bad, we know we're good.
Blowin' your mind like we knew we would.
You know we're just struttin' for fun.
Struttin' our stuff for everyone.
We're not here to start no trouble.
We're just here to do the Super Bowl Shuffle."

The solo lyrics were unique to each player. Payton sang, "They call me Sweetness" (and it sure sounds like he says "momance" when he means to sing "romance"). Willie Gault offers, "I dance a little funky, so watch me, girl." Linebacker Mike Singletary sings, "Give me a chance, I'll rock you good."

Jim McMahon starts with the line, "I'm the punky QB" for which he will forever be remembered. Linebacker Otis Wilson started, "I'm mama's boy Otis," and backup quarterback Steve Fuller says, "I run like lightning and pass like thunder." Defensive end Richard Dent may have had the funniest line when he sang, "If the quarterback's slow, he's gonna get bent."

William "the Refrigerator" Perry is the last soloist, and he sings, "I may be large, but I'm no dumb cookie."

The Bears went 15–1 in the 1985 regular season. Their lone loss was on a Monday night in Miami against the Dolphins. They filmed "The Super Bowl Shuffle" the day after the team's only loss. Some players who were supposed to participate did not do so because of the timing of the video. Dan Hampton and Steve McMichael, key members of the Bears' defensive line, did not attend the filming. Walter Payton and Jim McMahon, who were in the finished product of the video, did not do their parts on the day after the Miami loss, having their spots cut into the video after separate tapings.

The song earned a gold record, made the top 100 on *Billboard* music charts, and was nominated for a Grammy for Best R&B Performance by a Duo or Group. Gault, Richard Dent, and Mike Richardson attended the Grammys ceremony. Prince and the Revolution beat out "The Super Bowl Shuffle" that year with the song "Kiss."

The proceeds from the song and video went to a Chicago-based charity as set up by wide receiver Willie Gault, who was the mastermind of the entire affair.

The players did the video and recording without the knowledge of the Bears' front office. When team officials found out, they decided to let it go public rather than fight the players over their desired exhibition.

The video was played at halftime of the Super Bowl with the Bears up 23–3. How that affected the New England Patriots is unknown, but it certainly didn't get them any closer to winning the game.

39 1963 NFL Championship Game

From 1932 to 1946, the Chicago Bears won six NFL titles, and played and lost for the championship on three other occasions. During those 15 years, their longest dry spell away from the championship game was only two years. The Bears belonged in the NFL Championship Game as much as the Washington Redskins or New York Giants did.

But starting in 1947, the Bears went on a stretch of 16 seasons without an NFL championship. During that time, they played for the title only once, in 1956, when they were clobbered by the Giants 47–7 in the title game.

So when the Bears got to the title game in 1963 to again play the New York Giants, they were going for their first title since 1946. The city that had grown up with a Bears title every couple of years or so was dying for a chance to celebrate another football victory.

The Bears entered the game, and established themselves for decades to come as a superior defensive team. This one had re-adopted the name "Monsters of the Midway," a term given to the Bears from 1940 and 1941, which had been kind of pilfered from the old University of Chicago Maroons football teams from earlier in the decade.

The Bears had given up 144 points in 14 games (which, as most sports fans can figure, is 10 points a game, give or take). That's really, really good, in any era of football. That defense led the team to an 11–1–2 record, their lone loss coming at the hands of the San Francisco 49ers out by the bay.

Their opponent for the title game was once again the 11–3 New York Giants, who had scored 300 more points than the Bears allowed. They were led by one of the greatest passing quarterbacks of that time, Y.A. Tittle, who that season set an NFL record with 36 touchdown passes in 14 games. The Giants were playing in their fifth title game in the last six years, although they had not won a title themselves since that 1956 meeting with the Bears.

There was no surprise that the Bears and Giants were meeting in the NFL Championship Game. The 1963 game marked the sixth time since 1933 the two teams met for the NFL title. The Bears had a 3–2 edge in those games.

By the time the 1963 NFL Championship Game was over, the edge was 4–2 in the Bears' favor.

On one of the coldest days ever for an NFL championship game, played on the Bears' home turf of Wrigley Field, the Bears defense outdid the high-flying Giants offense with a 14–10 victory.

In 1963, the Bears were still eight years away from being forced out of Wrigley Field because it was too small for NFL audiences. They would eventually move to Soldier Field, the stadium on Lake Michigan. But in 1963, the NFL requested the Bears move the game to the bigger location so they could get more fans into seats. Bears owner George Halas turned down the request.

The game was televised by the National Broadcasting Company (NBC), but NFL rules blocked out viewers for 75 miles from the site of the game. To satisfy the local fans who could not get tickets to the game at Wrigley but wanted to watch it as it happened, the NFL and NBC set up three off-site closed-circuit telecasts of the game. There were 45,801 fans at Wrigley, and approximately 25,000 total at the three other sites.

What they saw was a Bears-preferred slugfest. The Giants scored first on a 14-yard pass from Tittle to Frank Gifford. The

Bears got that back on a two-yard plunge by quarterback Bill Wade following a 61-yard interception return by Larry Morris.

In the second quarter, Don Chandler kicked a 13-yard field goal because the Giants could not score from the 3-yard line on three plays. The Giants had a 10–7 halftime lead but they also had concerns over the health of 37-year-old Tittle, who had suffered a knee injury late in the first half.

In the third quarter, Bears defensive lineman Ed O'Bradovich intercepted a Tittle screen pass and ran it down to the Giants' 14-yard line. A few plays later, Wade had his second touchdown on a short run (set up by a 13-yard reception by tight end and future Bears coach Mike Ditka) and the Bears had a 14–10 lead.

The Bears made the score hold up through the fourth quarter. By the time the game was over, Tittle had thrown five interceptions (he had thrown only 14 interceptions all season long) and the Bears had their long-awaited sixth title since the inception of the championship game in 1933.

Linebacker Larry Morris was named the game's Most Valuable Player by *Sport* magazine. The Bears each received just under $6,000 for the victory.

The 17 years in between titles had been a long time. Little did anyone know it would be 22 years, and a major merging of the NFL and American Football League, before the Bears would win again.

40 The Standings

In 1932, the NFL had eight teams, including the Portsmouth Spartans (which would eventually become the Detroit Lions) and the Staten Island Stapletons (which eventually folded).

In 1933, the league got rid of the Stapletons, added the Boston Redskins, the Pittsburgh Pirates (that's right, Pirates), the Philadelphia Eagles, and the Cincinnati Reds and became a 10-team league. The league split the teams into two divisions, and the Bears became a member of the NFL's Western Conference, along with the Reds, the Green Bay Packers, the Spartans, and the hated Chicago Cardinals.

That Western Conference stood up, for the most part, until 1950, when the Cardinals moved into the Eastern Conference and the Bears were up against the Packers, the Lions, the Los Angeles Rams, the San Francisco 49ers, and the Baltimore Colts. Eventually, the Minnesota Vikings and Dallas Cowboys came along.

In 1967, the league had 16 teams and put them into four divisions. The Bears were in the Central Division of the Western Conference with the Packers, Lions, and Vikings.

In 1970, the NFL and AFL merged, creating a league that suddenly had 26 teams. They were split up into the American Football Conference and the National Football Conference, and each conference was then split into divisions—East, Central, and West. The Bears, Packers, Lions, and Vikings remained together, forming a bond that lasts to today.

In 1977, the Tampa Bay Buccaneers joined the NFC's Central Division, and those five teams battled each other twice a year through 2002, when the league found itself with 32 teams and a need to find a better arithmetical way to arrange them. They came up with two conferences of four divisions each, with each division having four teams. Once again, the Bears, Vikings, Packers, and Lions were together as they had been since 1961, this time in what was called the NFC North Division.

It was also called the Black and Blue Division, a name that had been applied from the 1960s because of the weather in those cities and the tough-hitting reputations those teams had. That name stuck through to the 21st century.

At the end of the 2019 season, the Bears had played the Packers 200 times, the Lions 180 times, and the Vikings 118 times. To contrast, they had 91 games against the Chicago/St. Louis/Arizona Cardinals, and 94 against the Los Angeles/St. Louis Rams.

41 Jay Cutler

The Chicago Bears franchise is unique in its origin, in its long history, in its overwhelming predominance as a quality defensive unit, and in its singular Super Bowl title.

But nothing is more unusual about the Bears than their bizarre history of unexceptional quarterback play.

In 100 years of existence, the Bears have only three Hall of Fame quarterbacks, and their most recent one was the best of the lot, Sid Luckman, who retired in 1950. In the 70 years that followed, the Bears never had a quarterback who could even prompt a "should he be in the Hall of Fame" conversation.

Their quarterback for the 1985 Super Bowl champions was Jim McMahon, the perfect QB for that team but not an NFL leader at the position. The quarterback for the team that lost the Super Bowl at the end of the 2006 season was Rex Grossman.

Jay Cutler celebrates a touchdown with Brandon Marshall during a 2014 game. (AP Photo/Paul Spinelli)

'Nuff said.

The 2008 season was played with Kyle Orton as the starting QB, and he was as well known for his "neck beard" as he was for his performance. He replaced Grossman at the position.

In the spring of 2009, general manager Jerry Angelo pulled off one of the most startling trades in Bears history, giving up Orton, a first and third round pick in the 2009 draft, and a first-round pick for 2010 to receive Jay Cutler, who played his college football at Vanderbilt and was a native of Santa Claus, Indiana.

In Denver, Cutler had proven to be a prolific passer, but failed to get the Broncos to the playoffs in two seasons as the starter. When team front office leadership changed after the 2008 season, Cutler became expendable and thus was traded to the Bears.

Chicago was ecstatic! They had a real threat as a passing quarterback for the first time since, well, maybe Sid Luckman. He wasn't always the most precise passer, but he could wing it, and came to town with a reputation as a quality QB. Few people argued over the loss of two first-round picks for a player of Cutler's caliber.

The relationship rusted almost immediately, as he threw four interceptions in his first start against Green Bay, and later that 2009 season he had a game against San Francisco in which he threw five interceptions with no touchdowns. His first season ended with a touchdown-to-interception comparison of 27–26.

The Bears coach at the time was Lovie Smith, who was a well-respected defensive coach but had no coaching skill on the offensive side of the ball. So, the Bears hired Mike Martz, a Super Bowl–winning coach with the St. Louis Rams, to lead the offense, and there again was a sense of promise in Chicago.

That 2010 team had an 11–5 record, made the playoffs, and even advanced to the NFC championship game against Green Bay, which they lost 21–14. Still, a Bears team had something akin to a threatening offense and the future looked promising.

It was at this point, however, that a peculiar characterization of Cutler began to take shape.

Cutler was a diabetic and had to monitor his blood sugar level even during games. In order to maintain his blood sugar level appropriately, Cutler had learned to maintain an even emotional keel: never too high or too low. Unfortunately, that even temperament came off as uncaring to Bears fans, who wanted to see some fire in their quarterback. Cutler was trained through his life not to let his emotions run too hot, and Bears fans grew accustomed to seeing him shrug off a poor play or drive rather than burst back to the sidelines or out onto the field to inspire the team.

Cutler also had difficulty staying on the field. He left the NFC championship game in 2010 with a sprained MCL and took a great deal of heat for that because there was no single play that seemed to have caused the injury. Through the years, he suffered a concussion, a groin injury, a thumb injury, and eventually a shoulder injury that caused him to miss the last half of the season. Through his eight-year career with the Bears, he played in 102 of 128 games, had a record of 51–51, and obviously never carried the Bears where they hoped they would go.

But he also ended his career with 14 team records, including most completions, most passing yards, most touchdowns, and the highest career completion record. He also owns the team record for most times sacked.

42 Bill Wade and Other Quarterbacks

Look at any NFL team that has been around, say, 50 years, back to the 1970 merger with the American Football League. Find somebody who knows something about every one of those teams, and ask them to name the best three quarterbacks that team has ever had. Probably every one of those experts will be able to give you the names of three quarterbacks and have an additional name of the fourth guy who was really, really good, too.

The Chicago Bears, however, have a meager history in terms of quarterback play. So much so that well into the 21st century, the first name mentioned when you talk about great Chicago Bears quarterback is Sid Luckman, who played in the 1940s and '50s.

Dating back to 1946, there have only been three championship Bears teams, which means there have only been three championship Bears quarterbacks. Luckman led the 1946 team, as he did title teams in 1940, 1941, and 1943. Jim McMahon was the spectacular and sometimes peculiar quarterback of the 1985 Bears Super Bowl team, and because of their singular dominant win in that game, and the massive impression that team left upon the NFL landscape, McMahon has his own star in the Chicago sports sky.

But McMahon would not be the second-best Bears quarterback in most eyes. That would probably be Bill Wade, who led the 1963 team to the NFL title at a time when the Bears had gone 17 years without a championship.

In 1962, Wade threw for 466 yards in a flamboyant 34–33 win over the Dallas Cowboys. But the Bears were not a strong offensive team in that era. In the 1963 title game, won by the Bears 14–10 against the New York Giants, Wade scored the Bears' two touchdowns on runs of two and one yards, an indication that there wasn't a lot of offense on a team that averaged just 14 points per game in that title season.

Luckman was the Bears' starting quarterback for 10 seasons. Wade started for only four seasons. McMahon was the starter for seven seasons but had the hardest time staying healthy.

Since McMahon left the team in 1988, quarterback play has been spotty at best.

Jim Harbaugh, who eventually would become head coach of the San Francisco 49ers, led the Bears for five seasons but had a difficult relationship with coach Mike Ditka. Erik Kramer, a talented passer, started for the Bears in 46 games over five seasons from 1994 to 1998. Rex Grossman started 31 games for the Bears over six seasons and got the team to the 2006 Super Bowl, but nobody will ever suggest Grossman was a great quarterback.

In 2009, the Bears acquired former Denver Broncos quarterback Jay Cutler, a known gunslinger, and Bears fans thought they finally had someone to challenge Luckman, but it did not turn out to be so through his first four seasons in town.

So let's go backward from McMahon to Wade. Bobby Douglass started 45 games for the Bears from 1968 to 1975, but he was best known for the fact that he could run the ball out of the quarterback position. He had the dubious distinction of a career total of 36 touchdowns and 64 interceptions, but in 1972 he set an NFL record for most rushing yards by a quarterback at 968 yards, to go along with eight touchdowns.

The only other great quarterback in the group was Johnny Lujack, who actually beat out Luckman for the starting job in 1949 after winning the Heisman Trophy while at Notre Dame.

But Lujack only started three seasons for the Bears before leaving the team and the game in a salary dispute with George Halas.

So, go ahead. Name the three best quarterbacks in Chicago Bears history. Start with Sid Luckman, and then....

43 Mike Singletary

It was the eyes.

Mike Singletary played middle linebacker for the Chicago Bears from 1981 to 1992. No position in football is as connected to the success of a franchise as middle linebacker is to the Chicago Bears, and Singletary took the responsibility of maintaining that standard with a singularity of focus. His intense nature on and off the field made him successful.

At six feet tall, Singletary was short by modern linebacker standards. He was also not particularly fast, a talent which is deemed necessary for success at the position in order to cover both charging running backs and tight ends crossing the middle of the field on pass patterns. But what made Singletary successful was the will he had to succeed, and his desire to do whatever it took to help his team win.

And you could see all of that desire in Singletary's eyes.

It became standard fare on telecasts of Bears games. A camera would be set at the end of the field Singletary would be facing from his middle linebacker position. As the play was being called by the offense, the camera would zoom in on Singletary's face. There, sitting smallish on his round face, were the wide, never-blinking, never-wavering eyes of Mike Singletary.

Richard Dent congratulates Mike Singletary on yet another big play.

After a stellar career with the Baylor Bears in college, when he was selected as an All-American in both his junior and senior years, Singletary was selected in the second round of the 1981 draft by the Chicago Bears. Halfway through his rookie season, Singletary earned the starting middle linebacker spot, a position previously held by some of the most famous names in football history, starting with the man who invented the position—Bill George—to the man who placed the stamp of intimidation to the position—Dick Butkus.

His eyes were a symbol of Singletary's focus on the field. Because of his intensity and unwavering attention to detail, he earned the nickname "Samurai Mike."

By 1985, Singletary was established as the heart—if not the soul—of the Bears defense that had earned all sorts of recognition. It was the Bears defense that led the team to its first Super Bowl appearance and victory, and Singletary was recognized as the best player on that defense when he was named NFL Defensive Player of the Year.

In the Super Bowl itself, Singletary recovered two fumbles as the team steamrolled the New England Patriots 46–10.

Singletary was also known for his ability to stay healthy enough to play. He missed two games in his career with the Bears, both in the same season. In his eighth season in the league, 1988, he was once again named NFL Defensive Player of the Year.

Singletary went on to become a coach in the NFL, starting out as a linebackers coach for the Baltimore Ravens, and after one season he became the assistant head coach and linebackers coach of the San Francisco 49ers. He eventually became interim head coach of the 49ers in 2008 and was given the head coaching position for the 49ers and coached them until the next to last game of the 2010 season, when he was fired.

Following the 2012 season, the Bears were looking for a new coach after firing Lovie Smith. Singletary was interviewed for the position, but the Bears instead hired Montreal Alouettes coach Marc Trestman.

44 1932 NFL Championship Game

The NFL got its start in 1920, but did not have a championship game until 1932. That season, the Chicago Bears had a record of 7–1–6, and the Portsmouth Spartans (the franchise that would eventually become the Detroit Lions) had a record of 6–2–4. The Green Bay Packers were 10–3–1. The league decided to have a final game to have a clear-cut champion. It was not marketed as a championship game; it was, instead, an added game to the regular season schedule.

The Bears and Spartans had played each other twice during that season and tied both times. The Bears, in fact, tied their first three games of the season by the score of 0–0. The Bears and Spartans managed to score when they played each other, tying the first time 13–13 and the second time 7–7.

There is no official explanation for why the NFL decided the Bears and Spartans would play for the championship and not the Packers. From the beginning, ties were discarded when determining a champion, and winning percentage was used as the final determinant. The Bears had a winning percentage of .875, the Packers had a winning percentage of .769, and the Spartans had a winning percentage of .750.

But because the Bears had only one loss and the Spartans had only two, it was determined that they were the two best teams in the league, and would play that final regular season game for all the marbles.

The game had to be played somewhere, and since the Bears technically had the better record, they were invited to host the game at their home field, Wrigley Field. Unfortunately, when it came time to have the game, Chicago was enjoying a particularly brutal week of weather. So the NFL decided to move the game to Chicago Stadium, home of the Chicago Blackhawks hockey team and eventually home to the Chicago Bulls of the National Basketball Association.

Chicago Stadium could not house a full 100-yard football field, so an 80-yard field was marked off. Prior to the game, the stadium had hosted a circus, and there was still the requisite dirt on the floor, so the game was played on the same stuff the elephants had roamed around in.

Because the game was indoors, and there were lights in Chicago Stadium, the game was held at night to allow for more fans to be able to attend.

There were unique aspects to the game beyond the site of the contest. The Spartans played the game without their best player, quarterback Earl Clark, nicknamed Dutch. He had a non-football job as coach of the Colorado College basketball team, and they had a game the night of the title contest. He did not play for the Spartans.

Meanwhile, Bears star running back Red Grange was kicked in the head in the first quarter and was knocked unconscious. He did not play again until late in the fourth quarter.

As one might gather from the scores of the earlier games, including the Bears' three 0–0 ties, there was not a lot of scoring back in those days. The Bears and Spartans played to a 0–0 tie through three quarters of this non-championship championship game.

Late in the game, the Bears gained momentum when safety Dick Nesbitt corralled a pass for an interception and ran it back deep into Portsmouth territory. At that point, Grange re-entered the game.

Grange's backfield running mate that year (and only that year) was Bronko Nagurski, a mountain of a man who played fullback.

Nagurski carried the ball to the 1-yard line, but on third down Nagurski was stopped for no gain by the Portsmouth defense.

On fourth down, the ball was hiked to Nagurski (this was in an era when the quarterback did not handle the ball on every down), and Nagurski made a move toward the stacked line of scrimmage. But then he stopped, faded back, and threw a jump pass to Grange in the end zone, who caught the ball for the game's only touchdown.

At that moment, controversy erupted. In 1932, the rules of the game stated that a forward pass could only be attempted from five yards or more behind the line of scrimmage, the Portsmouth coach Potsy Clark declared that Nagurski had not faded back far enough. The referees disagreed, allowed the touchdown, the Bears added an extra point and a late safety, and won the game 9–0.

The indoor game, known at the time as the "Tom Thumb" game because of its diminutive field, had two lasting effects on the game of football. The rule about the forward pass was altered, so that passers could throw the ball from anywhere behind the line of scrimmage rather than just from five yards back or farther.

Also, the 1932 "championship" game was the last one in which teams were required to line up from where the ball had ended up on the previous play. At the time, if a player was tackled along the sideline on the previous play, the next play started from there. After the '32 game, the NFL invented hash marks that would move the ball in from the sidelines 10 yards, allowing teams a bit more field for offensive flexibility.

Fifty-five years after the 1932 championship game, Arena football was invented, in which teams would play a version of football on tight 50-yard fields inside roofed stadiums. Unlike the Bears-Spartans game, Arena football was almost entirely a passing game, and it had scores that would reach the 60s and 70s.

45 Placekickers

It seems every sport has a player position of unusual effect. In baseball, the pitcher starts every play, and he has the opportunity to dominate the outcome.

Hockey has goalies. Soccer has goalkeepers. In each case, the player plays a dominant role.

In football, the ball is always put first into the hands of the quarterback, giving him a role similar to that of a baseball pitcher. The quarterback's ability to handle the handoff or the pass plays a major role in every play of a football game.

And yet, a remarkably high percentage of football games are determined not by the quarterback, but by a player whose greatest skill is the ability to kick the ball when it is not in motion—the placekicker.

The Bears' best placekicker is a topic of discussion, with at least three names offered for consideration. The most recent of those is Robbie Gould.

After failing to catch on with the New England Patriots and Baltimore Ravens following his successful collegiate career at Penn State, Gould was working construction when the Bears contacted him early in the 2005 season because they were in need of a placekicker. He played 11 seasons for the Bears, completed that time with an 85.4 percent accuracy rate on field goals, and was the Bears' all-time leader in career points (1,207), field goals made (276), and field goals of at least 50 yards.

At one point, Gould connected on 26 consecutive field goal attempts, breaking the team record previously held by Kevin Butler of Super Bowl fame. After his first two seasons with the Bears,

Gould was rewarded with a six-year contract that included a $4.25 million signing bonus, making him the highest-paid kicker in NFL history.

But he missed six field goal attempts in his final Bears season of 2015 (although he also made the most field goals in one season of his career) and new general manager Ryan Pace made the first of several questionable decisions by refusing to resign Gould, thus setting up one of the worst placekicking stories in team history.

Wait for it.

The first best placekicker in Bears history was George Blanda, a historic figure in pro football annals. He played 26 years in the NFL as a quarterback and kicker, which is what his job was when the Bears signed him in 1949 for $600. Blanda only played one year as the Bears' starting quarterback, but kicked 88 field goals and 247 extra points for the Bears in his nine seasons with the team.

Bob Thomas, who grew up in New York, kicked collegiately at Notre Dame, and that always plays well with the Chicago Bears, who picked him up in 1974 after he was drafted by the Los Angeles Rams. Thomas played for the Bears for eight seasons, then came back after a year with the Detroit Lions. He played 126 games for the Bears, and was extremely popular, never more so than when he made a 28-yard field goal with nine seconds left in overtime to give the Bears a 12–9 win over the New York Giants in 1977. That victory gave the Bears a 9–5 record that season, which was what they needed to make the playoffs for the first time in 14 years, and the first time since they won the NFL championship in 1963.

After retirement, Thomas went on to become a Justice in the Illinois Supreme Court.

Although Thomas made 22 of 28 field goal attempts in 1984 after his one season in Detroit, the Bears used a fourth-round draft pick in 1985 to grab a kicker out of Georgia named Kevin Butler. At the time the Bears knew they were on to something special (they would make the Super Bowl that season), and the young Butler beat out Thomas for the placekicking job. In his rookie season, Butler led the league in scoring with 144 points, making 31 of 37 field goal attempts and all 51 extra points he attempted that season.

In 1985, the Bears won 15 of 16 games, and the closest victory was a six-point win over the Green Bay Packers. There was one other seven-point win, and one nine-point win, but the rest were by double digits. Butler had no special duties other than converting the extra points when the offense got into the end zone.

Butler kicked three field goals in the Super Bowl win over the New England Patriots after the 1985 season. He played 11 seasons for the Bears, and when he was finally released, he was the last member of that Super Bowl team remaining with the club.

Butler was so revered in Chicago that he earned a nickname of honor. He was called "Butthead" (which was meant as a term of endearment) the entire time he played for the Bears.

Now, let's return to the end of the Robbie Gould story.

After 2015, Gould went on to play three seasons with the San Francisco 49ers, and in 2019 signed a four-year, $19 million contract with the team. At the end of the 2019 season, Gould played in his second career Super Bowl, hitting two field goals in the game to extend his perfect playoff streak to 15-for-15.

Why does Gould's success with the 49ers matter to the Bears?

They had unremarkable Connor Barth as their placekicker for the 2016 and 2017 seasons, but he made only 11 of 16 field goal attempts in 2017, and the team set up a summer-long competition for the job in 2018. The winner of that competition ended up being former Tennessee Titans kicker Cody Parkey, and his 2018 season with the Bears was memorable in all the wrong ways.

He made only 23 of 30 kicks during the regular season, and in the November 11 game against the Detroit Lions, Parkey missed four kicks (two field goals and two extra points), somehow managing to hit the uprights each time. Fans screamed for him to be replaced, but he remained on the team. However, fans were wary every time Parkey lined up for a kick.

After their 12–4 season, the Bears were in the playoffs for the first time since 2010, and the Bears trailed the Philadelphia Eagles 16–15 when they reached the Eagles' 26-yard line with time winding down. Parkey lined up a 43-yard field goal attempt that was tipped by an Eagles lineman, then bounced first off the left upright, then again off the crossbar, before falling in front of the goal, and the Bears had lost on what became known as the double-doink.

And Robbie Gould would kick in the Super Bowl for the 49ers the next year, with his perfect postseason record still intact.

46 Harlon Hill

Harlon Hill, one of the best receivers in Bears history, played his college football at tiny Florence State Teachers College, which later became the University of North Alabama. His performance in college was significant enough that he was invited to participate in a postseason all-star game in 1954, where he was seen by some NFL personnel, but not by Bears owner George Halas.

However, someone got it into Halas' head that they should consider adding Hill to their roster. The Bears, who have never been known as a home of good wide receivers, decided to use a

15th-round draft pick on the kid from Alabama without a whole amount of hope he would turn into anything.

They were wrong. Hill had a breakout season in 1954, catching 45 passes for 1,124 yards (an average of 25 yards per catch), for 12 touchdowns (an average of one per game). Although it was obviously an entirely different era, Jerry Rice, generally recognized as the greatest receiver in the history of the NFL, averaged 20.4 yards per catch in his best season as a pro.

In the sixth game of his rookie season, Hill caught four touchdown passes, two from quarterback George Blanda and two from quarterback Ed Brown, in a 31–27 victory over the San Francisco 49ers in San Francisco. He had 214 yards receiving in that game, a team record that stood until broken by Alshon Jeffery in 2013.

Hill had 42 catches and nine touchdowns in 1955 and 47 catches and 11 touchdowns in 1956 (with an average yards per catch of 24). His numbers began to drop by 1957, but he was still a scoring threat into the 1960 season.

Through the 2019 NFL season, Hill still ranked second all-time among Bears receivers with 4,616 yards receiving, behind Johnny Morris. But Hill played only 12 games per season, and he managed to play in every game through his first three seasons.

His career average of yards per catch was 20.4 and his 40 career touchdowns with the Bears is second among receivers to Ken Kavanaugh, who played for the Bears from 1940 to 1950.

Because he played his college ball at a small school, and became a stellar wideout in the NFL, the Harlon Hill Trophy was created in 1986 to give to the outstanding player in NCAA Division II, for schools smaller than the Division I schools. Since its inception, the award has twice gone to players from the University of North Alabama.

47 Walter Payton's Best Games

Walter Payton started his Bears career in 1975, and he was immediately placed in the shadow of Hall of Famer Gale Sayers, whose career had ended in 1971.

On October 30, 1977, Payton matched Sayers in one category, running for a team-record 205 yards in a 26–0 victory over the Green Bay Packers at Lambeau Field. He rushed for 117 yards in the first quarter of the game thanks to a 58-yard rush on one play. After leaving the game and the active lineup with 197 total yards in the fourth quarter, he returned to the game because he wanted to have a 200-yard game, and not because he was hoping to tie Sayers. But on his first carry he gained eight yards to reach Sayers' mark and coach Jack Pardee again removed him from the game.

It took Payton three weeks to improve on that mark and break Sayers' record.

On November 20, 1977, this time at Soldier Field, Payton had a day for the ages, rushing for 275 yards to set an NFL record. Amazingly, on that record-setting day, Payton only scored one touchdown, and it was on a one-yard run, in a 10–7 win over the Minnesota Vikings.

The previous record was 273 yards, set by legendary—and eventually infamous—Buffalo Bills running back O.J. Simpson in 1976.

The game that day was played in a swirling wind that became a signature of Soldier Field. As a result, there were very few passes thrown, which meant the Vikings were keying on Payton the entire game, as if that mattered. The Bears threw just seven passes that day, and Payton carried the ball 40 times.

Payton, it turns out, was feeling horrible that day. He had been battling the flu all weekend long, and reportedly his status for the game was up in the air until the day of the game, when he decided to give it a go. His temperature at game time was measured at 102 degrees.

Payton gained 29 yards on the game's first play from scrimmage. He had 144 yards at halftime, more than halfway to the record. With 5:38 remaining, he had 201 yards, and he broke his own and Sayers' record with a nine-yard carry right away. He then gained 58 yards on his 38th carry of the game, and eventually finished with 275 yards.

Payton deflected most praise for his effort and said his illness weighed on him throughout the game. "I just wanted to get that game over with," Payton said.

Payton's single-game record stood for 23 years until it was broken by Corey Dillon of the Cincinnati Bengals who had 278 yards in a game against Denver in 2000. (As of this writing, the record is held by Adrian Peterson, who gained 296 rushing yards in a 2003 game against the Chargers.)

When Payton retired, he held the league record with 16,726 career rushing yards. That record was broken by Emmitt Smith of

Walter Payton's Longest Run from Scrimmage

According to statistics listed at NFL.com, Walter Payton's longest run from scrimmage was 76 yards in a game against the Denver Broncos in October of 1978. The run took place at Denver's Mile High Stadium.

But Payton did have one longer run from scrimmage that NFL.com does not recognize. In 1979, in Philadelphia, Payton had an 82-yard run that actually ended at about the 1-foot line. But the play was called back due to an illegal motion penalty.

If you ever get a chance to see a video of the run, it is amusing to see just how upset Payton was to find out that his long run would not count.

the Dallas Cowboys in 2002. Barry Sanders of the Detroit Lions retired in 1998, 1,457 yards behind Payton and reportedly did so because he did not want to break Payton's mark.

48 Soldier Field Renovation

Walk south from the corner of Michigan Avenue and Wacker Drive in Chicago, and after about a mile you'll walk into one of the most attractive parks in all of urban America, Grant Park, bordered to the west by Michigan Avenue and to the east by Lake Michigan.

A few blocks farther south you'll see the Field Museum, a preserve of natural history artifacts and models. To the east of the Field Museum is the Adler Planetarium and the Shedd Aquarium. Slightly farther south of those structures is the home of the Chicago Bears, Soldier Field.

Back in 1924, when Soldier Field was constructed, the Greco-Roman style structure appeared as solid as the American soldiers it was designed to memorialize. Its initial capacity for football was 74,000. It was surrounded by seats on three sides and open on the north end, allowing for a unique view of downtown Chicago from inside the stadium.

Though some interior updates were made on the stadium over the years, the exterior remained the same. Gray, foreboding, majestic, rising above Lake Shore Drive on its west side, and statuesque when viewed from the lake. Solider Field was granted National Historic Landmark status in 1987.

That status lasted all of 16 years, and did not survive the renovation of Solider Field that made it into what it is today, a combination of modern glass and steel and historic stone and monuments.

The renovation came about after the Bears exasperated all of their attempts to find other places to play. They talked about the western suburb of Hoffman Estates, which was nothing but cornfields in the 1960s but had become a significant bedroom community by the 1980s. They talked to Aurora, a southwestern community that would eventually become the second largest population center in the state behind Chicago.

And they talked to Northwest Indiana, which had room at the border to the south end of Lake Michigan. But those grandiose plans were nixed by politicians, and the Bears stayed put.

Finally, in 2001, the Chicago Park District began the process of renovating Soldier Field, which needed expanded luxury boxes for high rollers, updated concession stands, and all the other amenities that new stadiums in almost every other football city in America (with the possible exception of Green Bay) already had. In some communities, they were on their third new stadium for their NFL teams, while Soldier Field stood unchanged and unmarred by modern necessities.

The exterior of the stadium, considered to be the more historical portion of the structure, remained the same. The signs and sculptures signifying the memorial to American soldiers was to remain. The interior, however, was going to be entirely overhauled.

The process would take two years, including one full NFL season. The Bears moved their home games for 2002 and the preseason of 2003 to Memorial Stadium in Champaign, Illinois, home of the University of Illinois. That is where Bears owner George Halas went to school, and where he got the blue and orange colors from which he designed the Bears' uniforms.

While the exterior of the old Soldier Field remained intact, the outer appearance of the stadium changed dramatically. Rising far above the stone supports and old casing of the stadium is a very modern glass-and-steel construct, looking very much like a space ship that employed Soldier Field as a landing spot. Especially from the west, the appearance of the new stadium is discordant.

The interior, however, did indeed improve dramatically. Video screens everywhere, clean restrooms, cleaner concession stands, and easy access to all levels make Solider Field feel like a new, modern stadium.

The renovation, however, had two negative effects. The new amenities had to replace some old seats, and the seating capacity ended up being 61,500, making Soldier Field the smallest NFL stadium based on capacity. This kept Soldier Field from being considered as a site for the Super Bowl as the NFL began experimenting with open-air stadiums in northern cities with the decision to have the new stadium in East Rutherford, New Jersey, host Super Bowl XLVIII.

The second negative effect is that all of the changes altered the core of Soldier Field enough that the National Historic Landmark status was taken away from the stadium in 2006.

49 Brian's Song

Say the words "made-for-TV movie" to anyone who was an adult in 1971 and you will see them take on a grapefruit face.

They were all the rage in the 1970s, and they were often loaded with melodrama and performed by actors at the end of their movie careers, or known specifically for long or short TV careers. They were popcorn viewing—light, airy, and enjoyable to consume without any lasting effects.

Brian Piccolo runs for tough yards in a 1968 game against the Packers. (Courtesy of Getty Images)

But on November 30, 1971, made-for-TV movies took a giant leap forward with the release of the film *Brian's Song.* For anyone who saw it in its original release, that movie remains one of the most dramatic shows viewed in one's own family room. It was shown on ABC's *Movie of the Week,* and it was an historic television event.

The story of *Brian's Song* is the relationship between former Bears star running back Gale Sayers and his teammate, lesser-known fullback Brian Piccolo. Sayers wrote of their relationship, and the difficulty that came when Piccolo was diagnosed with terminal cancer, in his autobiography *I Am Third.*

As teammates, Sayers and Piccolo formed a bond that broke racial barriers. When the Bears decided they wanted players who play the same position to room together on the road, Sayers and Piccolo agreed to become roommates. That placed Sayers, an African American man, in the same room as the Caucasian Piccolo, making them the first interracial roommate pairing in the NFL.

The movie told of their early problems together, because Sayers was a shy, country kid from Kansas with a slight stutter, and Piccolo was a more urbane, and certainly more outgoing, kind of football player out of Wake Forest.

Although the movie did fictionalize portions of Sayers' story, the meat of the movie told this true tale—the two became friends, and then became close friends. Their wives became friends. They cared about each other as they worked together for playing time. Sayers became a star, Piccolo was his backup and defender through the good and bad times of their seasons together from 1965 to 1969.

The movie became significant, and touched the hearts of everyone who watched, as Piccolo began to lose weight, and Sayers tried to keep his best friend's spirits up. Eventually, the story reaches its key dramatic moment as Piccolo is diagnosed with embryonic cell carcinoma. From that point the story is about Piccolo trying to deal with his impending death and Sayers trying to deal with losing his best friend.

The film's most touching moment comes after Piccolo dies. Reflecting an event that actually happened, one month after Piccolo died, Sayers was given the George S. Halas Most Courageous Player Award, and at the ceremony, Sayers told the audience the award should have gone to Piccolo.

Billy Dee Williams, an accomplished actor who portrayed Sayers in the film, delivered exactly the line Sayers said the night of the Halas Award ceremony:

"I love Brian Piccolo. And I'd like all of you to love him too. And so tonight, when you hit your knees, please ask God to love him."

James Caan, who was just one year away from appearing as Sonny Corleone in the first *Godfather* movie, and who had made a personal promise not to perform on TV, played Piccolo.

Fifty-five million people watched the original telecast of *Brian's Song,* and the lore of this legendary tearjerker, of grown men crying like babies, started before the final credits had even finished rolling.

50 The Dolphins Game

For more than 40 years, the 1972 Miami Dolphins were celebrated as the only team to go undefeated through the regular season and all the way through the playoffs to the Super Bowl title. There were some close games in the 14-game regular season, and the two playoff games and Super Bowl VII results were all close, but the Dolphins won them all.

For decades after that magnificent season, the Dolphins players from that team would gather to celebrate when the last undefeated team every year lost for the first time, preserving their position in NFL history.

And so many members of that 1972 team were at the Orange Bowl on December 2, 1985, when the Chicago Bears brought their perfect 12–0 record into town to play the Miami Dolphins. Through the miracle of precognition, the game was played on a Monday night before a national television audience.

The Dolphins came into the game with an 8–4 record, but that didn't matter. The fact that the '85 Dolphins were being put in a position to uphold the greatness of the '72 team made this Monday night one to remember.

In the Bears' season opener in 1985, they beat the Tampa Bay Buccaneers 38–28. After that game, no team managed more than 24 points against the Bears that season, with the exception of the Dolphins, who led 31–10 at halftime on the way to an astonishing 38–24 upset of the Chicago Bears.

At 12–0, with the most dominating defense in NFL history, the Bears were like Elvis. Everywhere they went, they made news. They traveled well; it was just as hard to get a Bears ticket when they played out of town as it was to get one when the Bears were at home.

In 1985, the Dolphins were still coached by Don Shula, the same man who had coached the '72 team to its perfect record. Shula told the players before the Bears game, "There's a lot of Dolphin history on the line" to set the stage for the underdogs.

The Bears knew they were on *Monday Night Football* because of their popularity. They also knew the Miami Dolphins' history, and the players were aware that those '72 Dolphins players were on the sidelines, watching the game.

Unfortunately for the Bears, they weren't 100 percent healthy that Monday night. Quarterback Jim McMahon was out with a shoulder injury, and Steve Fuller was playing under center. It's hard to say whether that would have mattered, with the way the Dolphins dealt with the 46 defense that night.

The 46 defense the Bears used was predicated on pressuring the quarterback hard, lining up eight players in the box to give the opposing QB a lot to think about, a lot of points of attack to keep track of. Such a defense had to work going forward because the receivers were going to have to be covered by three or maybe four players as the linebackers surged forward.

The Dolphins took advantage of that defensive scheme. The reason they could do it while others couldn't is that Miami quarterback Dan Marino, a future Hall of Famer, had the moxie to stay in the pocket as long as possible without withering under pressure. He also had a stalwart offensive line that kept the Bears at bay.

Miami scored on its first five possessions that night; they had a 33-yard crossing-pattern pass from Marino to Nat Moore, and two Ron Davenport rushing touchdowns (the second one set up by passes of 52 and 26 yards from Marino to Mark Duper and Mark Clayton, respectively). Marino and Moore combined for another touchdown pass just before halftime, as the Dolphins scored four first-half TDs.

The Dolphins finished their scoring in the second half on a pass from Marino to Clayton that bounced off defensive end Dan Hampton's hands first.

There are coaches who believe teams need to be knocked down once, even on the way to a near-perfect season, in order to know what it takes to win it all. Of course, the '72 Dolphins didn't need that, but the Bears responded to the loss by winning their last three games and absolutely cruising through the playoffs and Super Bowl with shutout wins over the New York Giants and Los Angeles Rams before crushing the New England Patriots 46–10 in Super bowl XX.

The Bears did not want to play New England. The Patriots played Miami that season in the AFC Championship Game, but beat the host Dolphins 31–14 to advance to the Super Bowl, thus keeping the Bears from exacting revenge on the Fish from Florida.

51 "Bear Down, Chicago Bears"

From a historical standpoint, what makes the Chicago Bears stand out?

They were in the NFL before it was the NFL, although they went by the name the Chicago Staleys that first year. Their uniforms have stayed consistent through time. So has their emblem and helmet. Their most notable hero, Walter Payton, is a hero for the entire league as much as he is for Chicago. Their original coach and owner, George Halas, remains an active part of the league's nomenclature 30 years after his passing.

But the Bears have one thing that is unique among NFL teams. They have a fight song, recognizable throughout the country.

"Bear Down, Chicago Bears" was the first NFL fight song. It was written in 1941 by a man named Al Hoffman, although he is given credit for the song under the pseudonym Jerry Downs.

The song is sung after every Bears score at home games, whether it is a touchdown, a field goal, or a safety. The lyrics are pretty simple, but if you go to a game, don't worry because they are displayed on the scoreboards for you:

Bear down, Chicago Bears, make every play clear the way to victory.

Bear down, Chicago Bears, put up a fight with a might so fearlessly.

We'll never forget the way you thrilled the nation, with your T-formation.

Bear down, Chicago Bears, and let them know why you're wearing the crown.

You're the pride and joy of Illinois, Chicago Bears, Bear Down.

The song was written the year after the Bears crushed the Washington Redskins 73–0 in the 1940 NFL title game. The reason they won so overwhelmingly is that they used the T-formation, a new-fangled way of employing three running backs behind the quarterback that made it very difficult for the defense to know what was coming.

Why Hoffman wrote the song is unclear. He was a very well-known songwriter at the time. If you are not from the 1940s or '50s, talk to a relative about the song "Mairzy Doats" or the song "Hot Diggity" and you will know something more about Hoffman.

Today, some other NFL teams have their own fight song, but none of them carry the weight of history the way "Bear Down" does. Once you know the song, you will be surprised by some of the places and times that you will hear it, on commercials or on football-related video games.

52 Halas Retires

George Halas' coaching record is spotted, not with failure, but with interruptions.

Halas coached the Bears from 1920 to 1967, but not continuously. He stepped away from the coaching position three different times, until his final retirement press conference in May of 1968.

Halas coached the Bears from 1920 to 1929, becoming the team owner in 1921. In '29, at the age of 34, he left the field and let someone else coach the team, but he couldn't stay away long. He coached the team again from 1933 to 1942, when he entered the Navy to serve during World War II. After the war, he returned to coach the team again in 1946 at the age of 51 and coached until 1955, again stepping away from the sidelines for the 1956 and 1957 seasons. But coaching was in his blood, and he took over the reins again from 1958 through the 1967 season, when he realized at the age of 73 that he was no longer able to coach the way he wanted to.

And what was it about his coaching style that he could not continue at the age of 73? It was his relationship with referees that made him give it up.

"There was a strong temptation to continue for another season," Halas said at the press conference. "But looking at practical realities, I am stepping aside now because I can no longer keep up with the physical demands of coaching the team on Sunday afternoons. I have always followed the ball, and the officials, up and down the field."

By 1968, Halas' arthritis was such that he was no longer quick afoot, and coaching without being on top of the play, and the men in stripes calling the play, made Halas move away.

George "Papa Bear" Halas on December 13, 1970, doing his favorite thing: watching the Bears beat the Packers.

The Bears won Halas' last game as coach, 23–14, at Fulton County Stadium in Atlanta. Halas had a career coaching record of 318–148–31 in the regular season, a winning percentage of 68.2.

Assistant Jim Dooley took over the coaching reins after Halas' retirement, and George's only son, George Jr. (known as "Mugs"), was given the role of team president. Halas had been grooming George Jr. for years to take over when he was finally ready to move on.

Unfortunately, Mugs passed away in 1979 at the age of 54 due to a heart attack.

George Sr. returned to the Bears as team president (although, in some ways, he never really left), watching as the team's first general manager, Jim Finks, dealt with team issues. But Halas could not stay out of the picture entirely, and as the team failed

George Halas as Baseball Player

Before he was a professional football player, George Halas was a professional baseball player.

Halas played the big-three sports of baseball, basketball, and football at the University of Illinois. After graduation, he made money as a semi-pro and minor league baseball player. He was good enough to draw the interest of a scout for the New York Yankees and signed a contract to play major league baseball in 1919, before he signed his first deal with the Staley Manufacturing Co. to play football.

In a spring training game, he tried to stretch a true double into a wishful triple and injured his hip. He played for a few more weeks with the Yankees (12 games in all) but was damaged goods, at least in his ability to turn his hips to hit a baseball. He eventually ended his baseball career playing for a minor league team in St. Paul, Minnesota. He also played for the Staley baseball team in 1920, while serving as coach and player for the company's new football team.

Halas went on to play football through the 1928 season for the Bears.

to win enough on the field, Halas eventually went over his general manager's head and hired Mike Ditka to coach the team in 1982.

Halas died of pancreatic cancer on October 31, 1983, two years before the Bears got to their first Super Bowl.

In 2019, the NFL named its top 100 players from the first 100 years of the league's existence, as well as the top 10 coaches. Halas was one of those coaches.

53 Bears' First Game at Soldier Field

On September 19, 1971, the Bears succumbed to pressure from the league to move from 40,000-seat Wrigley Field to Soldier Field, which could hold 55,000 for football and even more for special events.

Soldier Field, the huge stadium on the south side of Grant Park bordering Lake Michigan, had hosted the Chicago Cardinals of the NFL for one season, 1959, before the Cardinals got permission to move to St. Louis. It also housed the Chicago Spurs, a professional soccer team, and the Chicago Rockets/Hornets, a minor league football team.

Soldier Field had also been the annual host of the College All-Star Game, a charity event between the best players from the previous college season who were preparing for a move into the professional ranks, and the reigning NFL champion.

Having the Bears as a steady occupant was a whole new ballgame, however, bringing seven home games a season, plus preseason games, to the stadium. Although the Bears had no intention of staying long-term, it was still a big moment for the stadium and the Chicago Park District, which owned the facility.

The opponent for the first game was the Pittsburgh Steelers. Soldier Field had received a facelift, especially on the field, where artificial turf had been put in to give the Bears solid footing through the tough fall and winter.

(The artificial turf at Soldier Field was removed in 1988 and natural grass was used from then on. As of 2019, the battle continued between the Bears, Soldier Field, and the NFL to get artificial turf put back in because the field is nearly unusable in late November and December due to the weather. But neither the Bears nor the Chicago Park District were willing to pay for the new surface or its upkeep, which is a large initial outlay but considerably less annually than dealing with natural grass.)

It was a pretty day for an opener, around 63 degrees, a light wind, and it was one of the most important games in recent Bears history, because the team had gone seven seasons without a title following the 1963 championship.

The Bears only gave up one touchdown on that Sunday, and it wasn't even given up by the defense. Pittsburgh's Preston Pearson picked up a goal-line fumble for a touchdown and a 6–0 Pittsburgh lead. The Steelers added three more field goals and Mac Percival gave the Bears one to set up a 15–3 score early in the fourth quarter. But the Bears got into the Pittsburgh end zone when Ed O'Bradovich forced a fumble by running back Warren Bankston and Bears linebacker Ross Brupbacher picked up the fumble and ran it back for a touchdown and a 15–10 score, still in favor of the Steelers.

Another Pittsburgh fumble forced by Hall of Fame linebacker Dick Butkus and picked up by O'Bradovich allowed the Bears another offensive possession. Backup quarterback Kent Nix, replacing benched starter Jack Concannon, led the Bears on a touchdown drive that ended with an eight-yard pass from Nix to wide receiver George Farmer; and like that the hometown record in their new home building was 1–0.

The Bears won their first three games at Soldier Field that season but finished 4–3 at home and 6–8 overall, with a five-game losing streak to end the season. There were talks aplenty about how to make Soldier Field better for football, as well as talk about finding a new home for the Bears, but the Bears stayed where they were for the next 40 years and beyond.

54 Richie Petitbon

The Bears in 1959 were coming off an 8–4 season in which they finished one game away from making the championship game. In the 1959 draft they selected Richie Petitbon from Tulane University, where Petitbon had been a quarterback and defensive back. He was destined to play safety for the Bears for the next 13 seasons.

Petitbon was a tremendous athlete. He was a state finalist in track and field in high school and made his original college intentions based on his desire to run track and field in college. Eventually, he wound up at Tulane, where he was a two-way player on the football team. He also returned kicks. But Petitbon relinquished his last year of college eligibility to play for the Bears, who drafted him a year before he was set to graduate.

He was also a more worldly and thoughtful football player than most. Well-read and well-versed in topics outside of sports, he was the thinking man's football player, which served him well both as a player and as a defensive coordinator, but not so much as a head coach, a job he held for just one year.

Bears coach and owner George Halas had no problem playing rookies if they could contribute, and Petitbon certainly could. As a rookie, Petitbon had three interceptions (one returned for a touchdown) and he had 10 total in his first three seasons. In 1962, his number grew to six picks and a touchdown, with an unheard-of average return of over 35 yards per interception.

Then came 1963, the year he put himself in the Hall of Fame with eight interceptions (and another touchdown) in the regular season. The Bears won their first title since 1946 in that 1963 season and Petitbon had an interception in the end zone on a late and too-long pass by New York Giants quarterback Y.A. Tittle that secured the victory. Petitbon also had a fumble recovery in the fourth quarter of that game.

Petitbon played through the 1968 season with the Bears, finishing with 37 interceptions and three touchdowns. His 37 interceptions are second on the team's all-time pick list behind Gary Fencik, who played on the 1985 Super Bowl team. Petitbon owns the team record for interception return yards with 643.

After retiring from playing in 1972, Petitbon joined the Washington Redskins staff in 1978 as the secondary coach, and eventually became the defensive coordinator, where he spent 11 years, earning him a place in the Redskins Hall of Fame (they call it the Ring of Honor). But in 1993, when the Bears were looking for a new coach, Petitbon made it very clear he was interested in moving up the coaching ladder and really wanted to do it with the Bears.

Instead, the Bears chose Dave Wannstedt, who was defensive coordinator of the Dallas Cowboys. The Redskins then lost their longtime coach, Joe Gibbs, to retirement, and Petitbon was elevated to head coach but was only in charge for one season, when the Redskins fell to 4–12.

55 Green Bay Packers

It is said you have to know your enemy to defeat your enemy, so here is what you need to know about the Green Bay Packers, the Bears' most hated and longest-running serious rival.

And let's be clear about one thing: Bears fans cannot be ambivalent toward the Packers. Bears fans do not dislike the Packers; they hate the Packers. They hate Packers fans. Although there have been many recorded instances of Bears fans marrying Packers fans, it is not a suggested path to a happy marriage.

Look up "Jokes about Green Bay Packers fans" and you will see a long list. (And don't tell anybody that the list of "Jokes about Chicago Bears fans" is equally long.)

Through the 2019 NFL season, the Bears and Packers had played each other 200 times in regular season or postseason play, the most of any rivalry in NFL history. To be a real Bears fan, you have to know something about the Packers, just so you can make fun of them.

So here is what every Chicago Bears fan should know about the Green Bay Packers:

In 1919, Curly Lambeau, a Green Bay native who played one year of college football at the University of Notre Dame, was working for a company in Green Bay called the Indian Packing Company. He and a friend, George Calhoun, decided one day to form a football team, to play against some of the other traveling teams around the Midwest.

The Indian Packing Company agreed to buy the new team its jerseys, and in return, the team became the Green Bay Packers.

Lambeau coached and played for the team in its first season, and was the team's representative in 1921 when it applied for and received a franchise in the new professional football league that had formed a year earlier. The NFL welcomed the Green Bay Packers into the fold for the 1921 season (which means the Bears have been in the NFL one year longer than the Packers, a key fact).

In order to fund the team, a group of businessmen from Green Bay formed the Green Bay Football Corporation, which provided needed capital for the club. The team has been "owned" by city residents ever since.

Lambeau played for the Packers for 10 years, then continued to coach them until 1949. He was George Halas' original rival from Green Bay, to be eventually replaced by Vince Lombardi.

The Packers won six of their 15 NFL championships with Lambeau at the helm.

Prior to the invention of the Super Bowl in 1966, the Green Bay Packers won 11 NFL titles, and twice won three in a row, something the Bears have never been able to do. The Bears, during the same time, won eight NFL titles.

Since the invention of the Super Bowl, the Packers have won four NFL titles, including the first two Super Bowls. The Bears have won only one Super Bowl, and they have a Super Bowl loss, which the Packers do not.

Here are some key figures you need to know to properly hate the Packers:

Vince Lombardi—Lombardi came over from the New York Giants to coach the Packers from 1959 to 1967, including the first two Super Bowls. He became Halas' new rival to replace Lambeau, and there are lots of stories about phone calls between the two men just to rile each other up. The Super Bowl trophy is named after Lombardi, while the NFC championship trophy is named after Halas.

Bart Starr—Quarterbacked the Packers for 16 seasons and coached them for another nine. The Packers won five titles with him at the helm. Not a bad guy, but he beat the Bears a lot of times in both roles.

Paul Hornung—He was a running back out of Notre Dame who played for the Packers for nine years. He played collegiately at Notre Dame, was the No. 1 pick in the draft in 1957, and also scored a lot of touchdowns against the Bears.

Brett Favre—Like Bart Starr, Favre played quarterback for the Packers for 16 years, from 1992 to 2007. Because the Bears did not win much in those seasons, and Favre won a Super Bowl and two NFC championships with the team, Bears fans are allowed to hate him most of all.

Charles Martin—Perhaps the most hated Packer, all for what he did in one game. A defensive end with a mean streak, he entered a game against the Bears in 1986 with a hit list of players he wanted to injure during the game written on a towel he wore at his waist. At one point in the game, well after the whistle had blown the play dead, Martin picked up Bears quarterback Jim McMahon and slammed him to the ground, injuring his shoulder, which was already less than perfect. McMahon was never the same thereafter.

There you have the basic information you need to hate the Packers. Have fun.

56 Johnny Morris

Just as it is true that there have not been a large number of great quarterbacks that played for the Chicago Bears, likewise there have not been a great number of wide receivers who left indelible marks on the NFL while playing for the Bears.

Back in the day, receivers weren't even called "receivers." They were offensive ends.

When Sid Luckman, the Bears' best quarterback ever, started with the team in 1939, he threw five touchdown passes in 11 games. Ken Kavanaugh had the team lead in scoring receptions with three. Luckman completed 48 passes that season. Kavanaugh caught six touchdown passes the next season.

Playing for the Bears in the 1950s, Harlon Hill caught 40 touchdown passes over eight seasons, an average of five per season. Although he may be the best receiver of the pre–Super Bowl Bears, he was still an offensive end when he played.

But in 1958, the Bears got one of their best receivers ever, and they really had to dig to get him.

Johnny Morris, a halfback and receiver from the University of California-Santa Barbara, was a 12th-round pick in the 1958 NFL Draft. Morris played 10 seasons for the Bears, and when he was done, he had the franchise record (which he still holds) for total reception yards at 5,059 yards. He also scored 37 touchdowns in his Bears career.

Morris could play behind the quarterback or out on the offensive line, but he eventually filled a role that was relatively new in the NFL. He would line up behind the offensive line but off to one side or the other, centered in a way between the quarterback and the tight end. The position became known as "flanker" (standing at the quarterback's flank, as it were), and he became one of the best ever at that position.

Morris joined the Bears with a reputation for speed, and he actually held a tie for the world record for the 50-yard dash at 5.2 seconds. In 10 years with the Bears, he scored 31 touchdowns as a receiver, five as a rusher, and one on a punt return. In 1964, he set an NFL record with 93 catches for 1,200 yards and 10 touchdowns. He was a key member of the 1963 NFL championship team, which was one of the most popular teams in Bears history because they were the last titleholder until the team won the Super Bowl following the 1985 season.

Television was exploding in the 1960s, and athletes were being used for their contributions to telecasts for pregame and postgame discussion. Morris began working for WBBM-TV, the CBS affiliate, while he was still a player in 1964, and he stayed with WBBM for 32 years, serving as sports director for many years and was the top sportscaster on the station for most of his time there. He was one of the first professional players to become the sports anchor for the nightly newscasts in the country. He also worked with CBS Sports on some football telecasts.

Morris, who had one Pro Bowl appearance and made the All-NFL team one season as a player, was honored more extensively for his TV work, and eventually was placed in the Chicago Television Hall of Fame in 2000.

57 Paddy Driscoll

In 1974, there was a movie named *The Longest Yard* about a football game between inmates and prison guards at a Texas prison. Late in the game, the prisoners stage a comeback, and score three points on a drop kick. The drop kick had virtually disappeared from American football in the 1940s, so the guards had never seen a drop kick attempted before, and weren't sure what it was, or how many points it was worth.

The greatest drop kicker of all time was John "Paddy" Driscoll, a former Chicago Cardinal and Chicago Bear who eventually became a confidant of Bears owner George Halas and replaced Halas as coach for a two-year period.

But let's get back to the drop kick, and make sure you know what we are talking about (assuming you haven't seen the movie).

A drop kick is essentially a field goal, but instead of the ball being held still to allow the placekicker to have an easy time connecting with the ball, a drop kick is exactly what it sounds like—the ball is snapped by the center to a player in the backfield, who drops the ball on the ground and as it bounces, kicks the ball through the uprights (hopefully). Although the drop kick was a scoring play when successful, it could come as a surprise to defenses who might have been expecting a run or pass since it did not require the same prepared setup as a field goal.

Back in the early years of the NFL, the football was much rounder than it is today. That made for a fairly satisfactory bounce. Driscoll could score on a drop kick like nobody else.

Driscoll attended his hometown college of Northwestern University, and while in school played for a short while with the

Chicago Cubs in 1917. After graduation, he played football for one year with the Hammond Pros (two years before the creation of the NFL). He also played for the Los Angeles Angels baseball team that year.

In 1920, he agreed to play for the Chicago Cardinals, who like the Chicago Bears were an original member of the NFL. He also played one game that year for the Chicago Staleys, who became the Chicago Bears the next season. Driscoll played for the Cardinals for six seasons and was their head coach for two of those seasons. Driscoll was a running back as well as a dropkicker and he scored 17 touchdowns for the Cardinals.

While with the Cardinals, he was credited with a 55-yard drop-kick field goal. In 1924, he scored 27 points in a game with four touchdowns and three extra points. In 1925, while still with the Cardinals, he connected on four drop-kick field goals in one game, an NFL record.

In 1926, famed Chicago Bears star Red Grange and his business manager C.C. Pyle decided to create his own football league called the American Football League to challenge the NFL (the AFL lasted one season in that incarnation). The Cardinals were afraid the AFL would try to sign Driscoll away and could not afford to keep him, so the Cardinals traded him to the Chicago Bears, who could afford him. Driscoll played for the Bears for four seasons, until retiring in 1929. He scored 14 touchdowns for the Bears.

In the 1930s, the football shape was changed to make it more aerodynamic for passing. That effectively killed the drop kick as a weapon because the ball was too unpredictable when dropped.

After his playing years, Driscoll served as the football coach at Marquette University in Milwaukee for four seasons, then became an assistant coach for the Bears from 1941 to 1956.

When Halas "retired" after the 1955 season, he turned the coaching job over to Driscoll, who coached the Bears in 1956 and

1957. The Bears reached the NFL title game in 1956 only to lose to the New York Giants 47–7, then slid to 5–7 in 1957, and Halas returned to coach in 1958. Halas gave Driscoll a front-office job and asked him to continue working as an assistant coach as well, which he did. He served in the front office until his death in 1968.

58 Coaches Between Ditka and Smith

Mike Ditka, who coached the Bears from 1982 to 1992 and led the team to its one and only Super Bowl title, was much beloved in Chicago. Despite often taunting fans and displaying an uncivil amount of anger, Chicago loved Ditka and Ditka loved Chicago. They were made for each other.

But the Bears went 5–11 in 1992, and Ditka had a testy relationship with ownership at that point. He was brought in to coach the team by Papa Bear George Halas, with whom he shared a father-son relationship. But Ditka did not get along with Halas' grandson, Michael McCaskey, who was running the team after Halas passed away.

But it was up to McCaskey to find someone to replace Ditka and that task was not going to be easy. He considered the popular tactic of brining in someone with Chicago Bear connections and thought about hiring former Bears safety Richie Petitbon, who had established himself as a talented defensive coach while with the Washington Redskins. But instead, McCaskey hired Dallas Cowboys defensive coordinator Dave Wannstedt.

Perhaps it was the mustache. Wannstedt, like Ditka, sported the signature facial hair under his nose, but he was obviously more of a defensive mind than the offensive-minded Ditka.

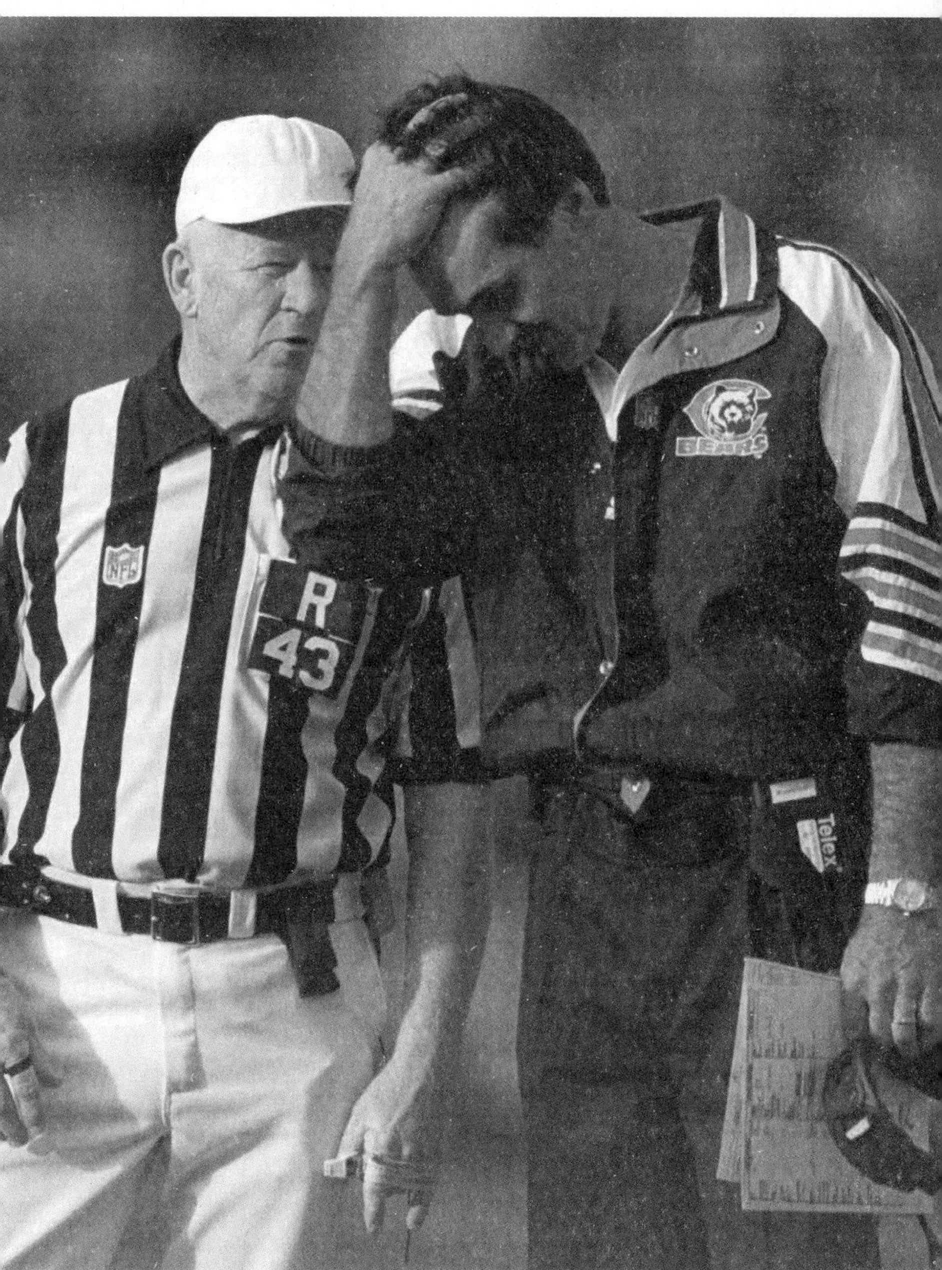

Dave Wannstedt listens to an official while showing the evident frustration Bears fans would come to know so well.

But Wannstedt never won much with the Bears. He improved the team by a couple of games in his first season, as the city came to know his Pittsburgh-drawl speaking style. The Bears made the playoffs in 1994 with a 9–7 record and won a playoff game, but lost a divisional playoff game to the San Francisco 49ers. Wannstedt won Coach of the Year honors, but that was Wannstedt's last playoff stop while with the Bears, and he was fired after a pair of 4–12 seasons, ending his run in 1998.

The next coach of the Bears was about as far removed from Mike Ditka as possible. Dick Jauron, a quiet, studious appearing man, was another defensive coordinator, this one from the Jacksonville Jaguars. A Yale graduate, he seemed to fit well with the bookish McCaskey.

Asked to improve the Bears from their 4–12 marks under Wannstedt, Jauron did that, by going 6–10 his first year and 5–11 his second year. He was actually under fire when the Bears caught fire in 2001, finishing 13–3 and winning the NFC Central for the first time since 1990. Two of the Bears' losses that season were to the hated Green Bay Packers.

The Bears were considered a strong NFC championship contender, but after a first-round bye they were surprised by the Philadelphia Eagles and lost 33–19 at Soldier Field. Like Wannstedt, Jauron got a Coach of the Year nod for 2001, but followed that with two losing seasons and was out of work after the 2003 season.

That's when the Bears found Texas-native Lovie Smith, who needed just three years to get the Bears back to the Super Bowl.

59 Coaches After Lovie

Coach Lovie Smith was one of the most successful NFL coaches to get fired, and one of the few to get fired after a winning season.

Smith was hired in 2004, replacing Dick Jauron. He joined the Bears after serving as the defensive coordinator for the St. Louis Rams, who went to the Super Bowl, and promised to return the Bears to prominence as one of the leading defensive teams in the league. He delivered on that promise, creating a defensive unit that led the Bears to their second Super Bowl in 2006. He ended up coaching the third-most games as a Bears coach behind George Halas and Mike Ditka.

But that Bears team severely lacked in offensive talent, and Smith was charged with finding someone to direct a quality offensive unit. He tried Terry Shea and Ron Turner and even Mike Martz, who was the head coach of the Rams team that made the Super Bowl with Smith on the staff.

Nothing really worked. After the Super Bowl season in 2006, the Bears had three mediocre seasons, followed by an 11–5 record in 2010 that ended in the NFC Championship Game. They failed to capitalize on that successful season, going 8–8 in 2011, and there was an unspoken mandate that Smith get the Bears back to the playoffs in 2012. He had only made the playoffs once in five seasons following the Super Bowl appearance and the fan base was wanting more postseason play going forward.

Smith came close to achieving that goal. The Bears started the 2012 season 7–1, but finished 10–6 and in third place in the NFC North, missing the playoffs because the 10–6 Minnesota Vikings had a better division record. Smith was fired after that season, having compiled an 81–63 overall record with the team, but only three playoff appearances in nine seasons. Despite being the most successful coach for the team since Mike Ditka, he was sent packing.

The Bears were historically a strong defensive team and a poor offensive one, and ownership wanted to change that reputation. Smith's last season was played under new general manager Phil Emery, and new GMs like to hire their own coach. Emery had been forced to keep Smith for his first season, but when the Bears failed to make the playoffs, a new coach was a foregone conclusion.

Who Emery hired was anything but a foregone conclusion, however. Looking for someone to jazz up the staid Bears offense. Emery went far afield, and out of the country, hiring Marc Trestman, the head coach of the Montreal Alouettes of the Canadian Football League. Longtime Bears fans were not pleased, although younger Bears fans thought an entirely new direction might produce the needed results.

Trestman had an impressive résumé, if one is impressed with success in the CFL. He was a two-time Coach of the Year and three-time CFL champion. His most impressive American football accomplishment was winning an NCAA title as quarterbacks' coach for the Miami Hurricanes, working with quarterback Bernie Kosar. He had numerous stints as a QB coach in the NFL, and as offensive coordinator for the San Francisco 49ers. In 1995, the Niners led the NFL in points scored and passing yards. He was also the offensive coordinator for the Oakland Raiders in 2002 when they lost in Super Bowl XXXVII.

In 2007, Trestman got his first professional head coaching job with the Alouettes. In 2013, one year after being interviewed for the head coaching position of the Indianapolis Colts, he was named head coach of the Bears.

Going all the way back to Red Grange, the Bears had a straight-forward power running attack, even though it often failed to produce well. Trestman came in and immediately changed the Bears offensive to a read-option offense, which promised better results.

Trestman also had some interesting coaching philosophies, including the concept that players from the offense and defensive needed to be acquainted with each other. He altered the Bears practice facility locker assignment so that offensive players and defensive players were interspersed throughout the locker room, rather than have a defensive side and an offensive side of the dressing room.

In his first season, Trestman led the Bears to an 8–8 record (two games below Smith's final season record of 10–6) but the Bears had the league's second highest scoring offense, and that had never been the case for any Bears team in the modern era.

In Trestman's second season, the Bears went 5-11, losing seven games by at least 13 points. Trestman and Emery were fired simultaneously following the 2014 season.

In the long history of the Bears (which is, in fact, the longest history in the NFL), they had *never* hired a head coach who had previously been a head coach in the league. After all, their two most successful coaches were Ditka and Smith. The formula of giving assistant coaches their first head coaching position had worked in the past.

But the Trestman experiment had been too weird for the city's broad shoulders attitude, and so the team hired former New Orleans Saints director of player personnel Ryan Pace to serve as general manager and longtime NFL head coach John Fox as head coach.

The two hires were concurrent, which was a problem. Most NFL GMs get to handpick their head coach, but Fox appeared to be assigned to Pace's first season. That relationship seemed strained, and played a role in Fox's short-lived career with the Bears.

Fox was as old-school as they came, and the team went 6–10 in the first season, 3–13 in his second, and 5–11 in his third. Pace's patience had reached its end, and Fox was fired with a record of 14–34 with the Bears.

Given the opportunity to make his own head-coaching decision, Pace found young Kansas City Chief's offensive coordinator Matt Nagy to coach the team in 2018. Which brings us to our next chapter, titled...

60 The Pace-Nagy-Trubisky Conundrum

Ryan Pace was hired away from his role as director of player personnel with the New Orleans Saints in 2015 to be general manager of the Bears. He was saddled with a new/old coach not of his choosing, veteran John Fox, and a quarterback nearing the end of his usefulness, Jay Cutler.

In the NFL draft in the spring of 2017, Pace traded two third-round picks and a fourth round pick to move up from third to second in the draft, because there were three highly sought after rookies on the draft block—DeShaun Watson from Clemson, Patrick Mahomes from Texas Tech, and Mitch Trubisky from North Carolina. Watson had a national collegiate title on his résumé, Mahomes was the NCAA's passing leader in yardage and touchdown passes, and Trubisky was a work-in-progress with only 13 collegiate starts.

Pace chose Trubisky with the second pick in the draft. The Kansas City Chiefs selected Mahomes with the 10th pick, and the Houston Texans grabbed Watson with the 12th pick.

Pace had set himself up for both immediate and continual player-assessment criticism with the Trubisky pick. Not only was he going to be questioned for picking Trubisky rather than Watson or Mahomes, he was endlessly mocked for giving up so many key draft picks to move up in the draft to get him.

The selection had ramifications for the Bears almost immediately. Trubisky did not start right away for the Bears. Mahomes played behind veteran QB Alex Smith for the Chiefs, and Watson started in his third pro game for the Texans and went on to earn a first-team all-rookie selection from the Pro Football Writers Association.

Like many veteran coaches, Fox was not interested in starting Trubisky right away, and the team settled on journeyman QB Mike Glennon, to whom they gave a massive free agent contract. Trubisky replaced Glennon as starting QB in the fifth game of the season. With Trubisky under center, the Bears went 4–8 in his rookie season.

Pace dealt with his coaching Issue by firing Fox at the end of the 2017 season after Fox went 14–34 in three seasons. Pace them hired young upstart Kansas City Chiefs offensive coordinator Matt Nagy, who was seen as a quarterback whisperer and an offensive genius ready to reinvent the game for the scoring side of the ball. He had worked with Mahomes in K.C., and with the Bears was assigned to turn Trubisky into a quarterback worthy of the No. 2 selection (and all of those draft picks).

During the 2018 season, it appeared Pace's decisions would bear fruit. The Bears went 13–3 in the regular season, Nagy was named NFL Coach of the Year, and Trubisky played well enough to avoid mistakes that cost the Bears games. He was not always brilliant, but he had one spectacular game, throwing a team-record six touchdown passes in leading the Bears to a 48–10 win over Tampa Bay. He finished the season with 3,223 yards passing, 24 touchdowns against 12 interceptions, and three rushing touchdowns. He matched the teams record for 300-plus yards passing in a game at four. The season was marred by the Bears home loss to Philadelphia in an NFC wild-card playoff game thanks

GM Ryan Pace (left) and head coach Matt Nagy (right) stand with superstar Khalil Mack following his acquisition. (Tim Boyle/Chicago Sun-Times via AP)

to the unfortunate performance of placekicker Cody Parker (see Placekickers, Chapter 45).

There were two other unfortunate aspects to the 2018 NFL season for the Pace-Nagy-Trubisky triumvirate.

Mahomes was spectacular as a full-time starting quarterback for the Chiefs in his second season, throwing for more than 5,000 yards, and becoming only the third NFL quarterback to complete 50 TD passes (joining Tom Brady and Peyton Manning). He was named NFL Most Valuable Player in 2018 in his second year in the league and first season as a starter. The Chiefs advanced to the AFC championship game, losing to New England.

And, remember, the Chiefs did not give up three draft picks to get Mahomes with the 10th pick in the draft.

And Watson? Coming off of an all-rookie season and late-season ACL surgery in 2017, Watson passed for 4,165 yards in 2018, had 26 touchdowns to only nine interceptions, and he had five rushing touchdowns. The Texans went 11–5 and lost in the wild-card round of the playoffs. And remember, the Texans did not trade away three draft picks to get Watson with the 12th pick in the 2017 draft.

The scorecard after one full season of the three quarterbacks all starting was Mahomes was the most spectacular, Watson was a dual threat, and Trubisky's team had the best team record. The 2019 season promised to tell the tale on both the Nagy and Trubisky picks for Pace.

Unfortunately: the Nagy-Trubisky relationship had a problem. Nagy was a pass-first, pass-second, and pass-third coach with little interest in running the football. That made any draw play meaningless because opponents knew the running back was not taking the handoff. Nagy also wanted his QB to stand in the pocket, and Trubisky was a more efficient passer while on the run. That conflict shone through the first half of the Bears' 2019 season, as the Bears started 3–2 through five games, including an embarrassing loss to a poor Oakland team in London in Week 5, which started a four-game losing streak.

The Bears were fortunate to stay in the playoff hunt until Week 15 but finished the season 8–8, as Trubisky threw for 17 touchdowns with 10 interceptions. He also had two rushing touchdowns.

Mahomes, meanwhile, led the Chiefs to the Super Bowl championship and Watson led the Texans to the AFC title game.

By all accounts, the 2020 season was described as a true test of the Nagy-Trubisky working relationship (although many fans were calling for Trubisky to be replaced) and the success of that relationship promised to weigh heavily on the perception of Pace as a talented and successful general manager and Nagy as the quarterback whisperer he was touted as.

61 GMs Finks, Vainisi, Angelo

If ever a man had the right to be hands-on in his managerial style, it was George Halas. He created the Chicago Bears, and everything that happened with the Bears not only bore his signature but affected his reputation. Halas was consumed by the Bears, and nothing slipped by him. That's why they had as much success as they did under his leadership.

Halas kicked himself upstairs for the last time in 1967, after he coached the Bears to a 7–6–1 record. He remained active in the organization as its owner, although he had turned the day-to-day workings of the shop over to his son, George Halas Jr., affectionately known as "Mugs."

In 1975, Mugs Halas decided to move the Bears into the same part of the 20th century the rest of the league was in and got George Sr. to allow him to hire a general manager to handle the on-the-field decisions while Mugs handled the business end.

The Bears got lucky that year because Jim Finks, an accomplished general manager with the Minnesota Vikings for 10 years, had a falling out with the club and was available for the Bears.

Finks came to the Bears having just won the NFL's Executive of the Year Award. In his decade with the Vikings, he helped create the team that would go to four Super Bowls from the 1969 to the 1977 seasons. Finks had drafted Hall of Famers like Carl Eller and Alan Page to the Vikings, as well as hiring head coach Bud Grant, who he got from the Canadian Football League.

Finks proved to be a wise choice as the first general manager of the Bears (he also had the title of executive vice president). He found, either through draft, trade, or other acquisition, 19 of the 22 starters who played in Super Bowl XX following the 1985 season.

But Finks was not with the team to enjoy that unbelievable season, because he resigned in 1982 when Halas Sr. went over

Ted Phillips

A number of men were allowed to coach the Bears while George Halas was running the team. But it was many years after Halas died in 1983 that someone outside the Halas family was allowed to run the team.

Ted Phillips was a longtime employee of the Bears and had reached the position of vice president of operations when Michael McCaskey, Halas' grandson, stepped down as president of the team in 1999. Phillips was promoted to president and chief executive officer, making him the first person outside the Halas family to be placed in that position of authority.

Phillips started with the Bears as the team's comptroller, then moved on to director of finance. As of 2019, Phillips remained the team president.

his head and hired former Bears tight end Mike Ditka as the new coach. Finks saw that as a general manager's duty, and left, signing with the Chicago Cubs to serve as president in 1983. Finks was team president of the Cubs when the team won the National League Eastern Division title in 1984.

He returned to the NFL in 1986 to serve as general manager of the New Orleans Saints. He was placed in the Pro Football Hall of Fame in 1995.

Finks left the Bears in 1982, and just before Halas Sr. died in October of 1983 the team hired their second general manager, Jerry Vainisi, who had served as the team treasurer for 11 years. Vainisi oversaw the completion of Fink's work in creating the Super Bowl–champion Bears but was fired by the team in 1986.

The Bears went 15 years without a general manager after Vainisi was fired. In 2001, the Bears hired Jerry Angelo, the director of player personnel for the Tampa Bay Buccaneers. Angelo helped put together the defense that carried the Bears to Super Bowl XLI following the 2006 season.

62 Bear Weather

Major League Baseball teams love to visit Chicago in the summer months. Three or four days in town to enjoy the shopping, the dining, the nightlife, and the beauty of Lake Michigan sounds like a decent assignment. In fact, Chicago teams believe they enjoy a distinct home-field advantage because visiting teams have so much available to them in terms of distractions when they visit the Windy City.

Although they don't spend as much time in town as baseball teams do, players from visiting teams in the NBA and NHL circle their Chicago visits for the same reason. It's a destination that stands out among the other urban experiences they have through a long season over the winter. It helps that they play their games indoors.

Football teams play outdoors, and once the calendar flips over to November and December, Chicago can be an unfriendly place to play. When the wind blows into Soldier Field, dropping the temperature sometimes from freezing to well-below when you consider the wind-chill, it's just not a great assignment.

For a long time, the Bears believed they had a distinct advantage over visiting teams from outside their division because they had to play in Chicago on a cold day on a cold field. The Bears, for their part, looked to the weather report in hopes Mother Nature would provide them with Bear Weather.

Bear Weather may not have had its effect on the Green Bay Packers, Minnesota Vikings, or Detroit Lions (although the Lions moved indoors for their home games in 1975 and the Vikings moved indoors in 1982), but when the Tampa Bay Buccaneers or Los Angeles Rams found their way to the lakefront, it was always helpful to have a cold wind blowing and temperatures down to where visiting players had to make sure they still had all their fingers on their hands because they could not feel them.

The coldest game ever played at Soldier Field was December 18, 1983, when the game-time temperature for the contest between the Bears and Packers was 3 degrees. The windchill was down to minus-15. The Bears won the game 23–21.

A couple of seasons removed from the Super Bowl campaign of 1985, the temperature was 4 degrees when the Bears hosted the Washington Redskins on January 10, 1988, in a divisional playoff game, but the home team lost 21–17.

There were even a couple occasions when Bear Weather was too "bear-like" to play the game outdoors. The 1932 NFL Championship Game between the Bears and Portsmouth Spartans (who soon became the Detroit Lions) had to be moved to Chicago Stadium because of sub-zero temperatures and the remnants of a recent blizzard.

Wrigley Field could be a cold place too (still is, some days) and the Bears played there until 1971. The 1937 Championship Game between the Bears and Washington Redskins was played at the temperature of 15 degrees with a 12-mile-per-hour wind. The Redskins prevailed 28–21 in that game.

Obviously, Bear Weather was not infallible. In the 1988 NFC Championship Game against the San Francisco 49ers, the Bears were pleased to see that the opening temperature sat at 17 degrees and the wind brought the "feels-like" temperature down to 26 below zero. The 49ers handled the cold better than the Bears and won easily, 28–3.

Heading into the 21st century, the idea of Bear Weather had sort of been given a pass. It turns out being from Chicago doesn't make one immune to the effects of cold. However, the weather did affect the games at Soldier Field as continuing problems with trying to grow natural grass in November and December created some very messy fields in those months.

63 Manhole Covers

George Halas was a very frugal man. He saved his money in his youth so he could attend the University of Illinois. When he got involved with professional football and owned his own team, the Chicago Bears, he followed every penny, keeping expenses down whenever he could.

He developed a reputation as a cheapskate, a miserly owner who would not give a player a single penny he didn't have to.

There are dozens of stories told about Halas negotiating tough deals with players, and a number of those stories end with players leaving the team, and in at least one case, leaving football. Former Bears quarterback Johnny Lujack stopped playing after a bitter negotiation with Halas. Mike Ditka, the former player and coach who is one of the most famous and beloved names in Bears history, became a former Bear during his playing days because of a bitter battle over money with Halas.

It was at that time that Ditka put voice to one of the great quotes of all time, when he said Halas "throws nickels around like manhole covers."

The negotiating part of Halas' legacy does not detract from the numerous cases of largesse and kindness Halas showed to players over the years. Perhaps the most famous case was the care with which he helped fullback Brian Piccolo and his family as Piccolo went through his battle with cancer.

But Halas was a notorious negotiator, and famously kept a list of transgressions his players made on the field (and sometimes off the field) to throw back at them when they requested money. Sid Luckman, the best quarterback in Bears history to this day, came to Halas asking for a $1,000 bonus after he led the Bears to the 73–0 shellacking of the Washington Redskins in the title game that year. Halas pulled out his sheet, detailing interceptions Luckman had thrown during the season, and gave him $250 as a bonus.

George Blanda, who played for the Bears before making his real name with the Oakland Raiders, was signed by Halas for the 1949 season and Halas gave Blanda a $600 signing bonus. When the season began, Halas demanded the money back.

Doug Atkins, a Hall of Fame defensive end who played for the Bears in the 1950s and 1960s, fought with Halas continually over money. Eventually, Atkins asked for a trade because he could not ever seem to agree with Halas over his salary.

Dick Butkus came to the Bears as a local hero, having grown up in Chicago, playing high school ball on the south side of town, and then attending the University of Illinois. But his career ended in 1973 when knee injuries kept him out of the game. He ended up suing the Bears, claiming they made him play even though they knew he was injured.

In an interview in the *Chicago Tribune* many years later, Butkus said negotiating with Halas was difficult. "He would say, 'I don't know what you think, but everybody comes here to watch Gale [Sayers] play, not you.' Then I talked to Gale later, and Halas had said to him, 'They're not coming to see you, they're coming to see Butkus.'"

Halas did make some players wealthy. He was one-third of a business group that allowed Red Grange to make upwards of $200,000 for two football tours across the country after he finished playing at the University of Illinois in 1925. He paid Paddy Driscoll $10,000 a year later after buying his rights from the Chicago Cardinals for $3,500.

But he also spent 40 years as owner of the Bears refusing to pay for a coach. He did that job himself.

64 Bears on Monday Night

Since the dawn of the televised sports age, the Chicago Bears have always delivered terrific national ratings. Bears fans are everywhere, and they like seeing their favorite team on TV, whether they are being watched in Los Angeles, Miami, Boston, or maybe even Green Bay.

That's one of the reasons the NFL bends over backward to get the Bears on their most popular national telecast, the *Monday Night Football* game.

Monday Night Football has been a staple of the NFL since 1970, when the league signed its first contract for the weekday game with the American Broadcasting Company. The game was moved to ESPN in 2006.

Through the 2019 NFL season, the Bears had been on MNF 68 times, with a record of 30 wins and 38 losses. The Bears ranked eighth among all NFL teams for appearances on *Monday Night Football.*

Every Monday night game is a happening in the towns represented by the two teams. But the entire nation enjoyed the Bears' Monday night game on October 16, 2006, when Brian Urlacher and Devin Hester both showed the NFL audience what they could do when given the opportunity to do so.

The Bears entered that game as the favorite to win the NFC and move on to the Super Bowl. The Bears were 5–0 heading into that game, and that's why it was so surprising that the Cardinals opened up a 23–3 lead in the third quarter.

Well, maybe it wasn't surprising. Quarterback Rex Grossman was having a Grossman of a day, with four interceptions and two fumbles. It looked to everyone like the Bears were going to taste their first defeat.

But that's when Urlacher started knocking the ball out of the Cardinals' hands so that it ended up in the hands of Charles Tillman and Mike Brown for defensive touchdowns. Then, with the Cardinals crumbling and the Bears needing one more break, rookie Devin Hester returned a punt 83 yards to give the Bears a thrilling 24–23 victory.

The game was well-known for its on-the-field heroics, but it became more famous for the postgame interview by Arizona coach Dennis Green who proclaimed, "The Bears are who we thought they were!" in one of Chicago's favorite opposing coach rants.

Another famous Monday night game came on October 21, 1985, as the Bears were heading toward the Super Bowl (just like they were in 2006). Once again, a rookie played a big role, in this case a really big role, when 320-pound defensive tackle William "the Refrigerator" Perry was moved to the fullback position to score a one-yard touchdown in the Bears' 23–7 win over the rival Green Bay Packers. Walter Payton also scored twice, both times by following Perry through the offensive line and into the end zone.

In 1987, the Bears recorded eight sacks against the New York Giants for a 34–19 win. Almost 20 years before Hester made his notice with a long punt return for a score, Dennis McKinnon had a 94-yard punt return for a touchdown in the game against the Giants.

65 Other Homes for Bears

After the 1970 NFL season, the Chicago Bears were told to move out of Wrigley Field. Its capacity was too small for football, and many of the seats for football were temporary just to create a larger attendance.

The Bears immediately considered moving to Soldier Field, the large stadium on the south side of the city's downtown area, but Bears owner George Halas was not thrilled with the idea of working with the city of Chicago, which owned Soldier Field through the Chicago Park District. Instead, Halas wanted the Bears to play at Dyche Stadium on the campus of Northwestern.

A deal was struck between Northwestern and the Bears, but the Big Ten Conference, of which Northwestern was (and is) a member, struck down the deal, saying the playing field for any of its members' football teams had to be used solely by the university's representative team from the start of the football season to its end. Obviously, the college and NFL seasons run concurrently, although the NFL season runs much longer.

The Bears were allowed to play one game at Dyche Stadium, the first game of the 1970 season, but that game against the Philadelphia Eagles was the only one they ever played there. City residents put up a squawk about the Bears moving there permanently, and that idea was pushed aside.

With no other viable options, the Bears moved into Soldier Field in 1971.

The Bears, however, did not consider Soldier Field the long-term solution to their housing needs. From the first season, attempts were made to find a new home. When Halas signed the contract with the city of Chicago to play at Soldier Field in 1971, he did so with the belief that there were plans to build a stadium specifically for the Bears and that it would be ready by 1974.

In the 1960s, Mayor Richard J. Daley made several attempts to build a new home for the Bears. There was consideration for tearing down Soldier Field and building a new stadium just to the south of Soldier Field. Two other sites within city limits were being considered, including one to the east of Chicago Stadium on Madison Street on the city's west side. Eventually, it was decided it would cost the city about half as much to renovate Solider Field as it would cost to build a new stadium.

In the 1970s, as the Bears were returning to wide popularity with the inclusion of running back Walter Payton, Halas was talking about moving the team out of Chicago entirely and to the new bustling northwest suburb of Arlington Heights, which already had the popular Arlington Park Racetrack. Discussions got serious enough that at one point Mayor Daley told Halas that if he moved the team, he would not be allowed to call it the "Chicago Bears."

In 1985, a proposal was floated for a dual-stadium plan on the west side of Chicago near Chicago Stadium (then home of the Bulls and Blackhawks). The stadiums would have shared a roof, which could be rolled from one stadium to the other. The Bears would play in the football stadium, and the Chicago White Sox and Chicago Cubs would share the baseball facility.

None of the professional sports teams ever agreed to move, and the idea never moved past the design stage.

In 1989, after the two ideas for the west side were shot down by state legislators, Bears president Michael McCaskey, Halas' grandson, again considered moving out of the city of Chicago. The Bears had property options in a northwest suburb named Hoffman Estates, as well as in the western suburb of Aurora. But they never pulled the trigger on either option.

Move ahead to 1995, when McCaskey announced that he had an agreement with a group of developers in Northwest Indiana to construct a complex of structures, including a new stadium, and the area was to be called "Planet Park." Unfortunately, again, the plan ran into political problems when it was rejected by the Lake County, Indiana, Council.

Through all the years, Soldier Field kept getting minor facelifts. But in 1998, Mayor Richard M. Daley, son of Richard J., suggested the Bears move into Comiskey Park and share it with the Chicago White Sox. That plan was nixed by the Bears.

In 1998, McCaskey again went shopping for a new home and signed an option to purchase 69 acres of land in Elk Grove Village, a town just outside the city and surrounding O'Hare Airport. Once again, city residents hated the idea, but before it could be put to any kind of vote, the Bears pulled out of the plan.

Finally, in November of 2000, an agreement was reached that would put Soldier Field under a $587 million renovation that would create new luxury boxes, allowing the Bears to keep up with the other NFL teams in terms of revenue streams. The renovation also included a new parking garage and new park land around the stadium. Construction began in January of 2002, forced the Bears out of Soldier Field for the 2002 season (they played at the University of Illinois in Champaign) and was completed in time for the start of the 2003 season.

That renovation put an end (at least temporarily) to talk of moving the Bears out of Soldier Field.

66 Grass or Turf

Soldier Field, home of the Chicago Bears, is an imposing structure. With its granite colonnades on the outside, and its new modern glass-and-steel construct rising above the original bowl, it stands as a testament to the city's greatness.

But it is in Chicago, and it does host outdoor football games. Football is played on grass of some sort, and at Soldier Field, as of 1988, that grass was natural.

Natural grass has extreme difficulty growing after the first of November in the Chicago area. As a result, the Soldier Field playing surface is often thinned of grass, or missing grass entirely. On pretty fall days, it's mostly dirt. On wet fall days, or early winter days when snow has fallen, the field can be wet dirt, which is also known as mud.

Natural grass is not the only alternative. By the 21st century, most NFL teams were playing on an artificial grass surface known as FieldTurf, or one of its similar competitive surfaces. An artificial grass surface would cost millions to install, but would require much less maintenance than the grass surface does (the Chicago Park District regularly installs new sod during the Bears season to make the field playable in the later months of the season).

But the initial outlay of expense, estimated at $1.5 million in 2009, has been argued between the city and the Bears, and as of 2013, had not happened. The Bears have contended that their players prefer natural grass, and enjoy the home-field advantage of being more familiar with the surface than visiting teams.

When the Bears initially moved into Soldier Field in 1971, the surface was changed from natural grass to AstroTurf, the first widely-used artificial grass surface. AstroTurf looked nice, and was easy to care for, but it was not a pleasant surface to run on, and in 1988 the Soldier Field surface was changed back to natural grass.

In 2011, the Bears were scheduled to hold a practice session at Soldier Field in August as a part of a fan function. Fans paid to see the Bears practice, and then were supposed to have time to get autographs with the players. But when the Bears got to Soldier Field, they found the field unplayable (a recent concert had been held there) and the team left, creating a horrible public relations disaster for both the Chicago Bears and the city of Chicago.

Later that year, Bears president George McCaskey said that the grass/turf issue was not a matter of cost but of player safety, saying studies indicated players suffered lower leg injuries at a higher rate on artificial turf.

But Bears players, including superstars like Brian Urlacher and quarterback Jay Cutler, openly complained about the surface, and suggested it was holding up their best offensive players because of poor footing. But those complaints fell on non-responding ears.

The Bears and the Park District continued to study the issue, as more and newer and safer alternatives were being created. But the Bears played on grass, or what was left of it, in 2012 and there were no plans to change for the 2013 season.

67 The McCaskey Family

"Papa Bear" Halas had two children, a daughter, Virginia, and a son, George Jr., who became known as "Mugs." Mugs was groomed to be George Sr.'s replacement atop the Chicago Bears organization, but died suddenly in 1979 from heart complications. That left Virginia to run the team with the help of her husband, Ed McCaskey.

In 1983, when George Senior died, Virginia installed her son Michael McCaskey as team president. Although McCaskey had played football while at Yale University, he was not immediately thrilled with the prospect of running a football team, but he stayed in the position until 1999, when he made a rather public management mistake and was removed from the position.

Michael McCaskey and popular Bears coach Mike Ditka could not have been more different, and their differences led to some infighting that eventually became "out" fighting, as everyone in Chicago knew they were clashing. McCaskey fired Ditka in 1992 and replaced him with someone with whom he could work, former Dallas defensive coordinator Dave Wannstedt.

When Wannstedt could not produce a consistent winner, the Bears had to find another new coach in 1998 and McCaskey wanted former Bears assistant coach Dave McGinnis, who at the time was an assistant coach with the Arizona Cardinals. But McCaskey scheduled a press conference to announce McGinnis' signing before a contract deal had been reached, and McGinnis balked at signing with the team. The public relations mess caused by the miscue eventually forced the Bears to remove Michael from the role of team president. Ted Phillips, a non-family member who worked for the Bears, was placed as team president.

Michael McCaskey was made chairman of the board, replacing his father, Ed, who died in 2003. In 2011, Michael was replaced as chairman by his brother, George, who had far more interest in running the Bears than Michael, anyway.

When the Bears won the NFC championship in 2006, it was Virginia McCaskey, then 84 years old, who accepted the trophy, which is named after her father, George Halas Sr.

Virginia and Ed McCaskey had 11 children, eight boys and three girls, and dozens of grandchildren. Eighty percent of team

Michael and Virginia McCaskey react as they are handed the George Halas Trophy after the Bears won the NFC Championship Game against the Saints to advance to Super Bowl XLI.

ownership remained within the Halas-McCaskey family. Virginia remained the titular head of the family, and its family business, although she always swore she let the men in the family deal with football.

A story written for Drexel University in honor of Virginia McCaskey, a graduate of Drexel, asked George McCaskey if his mother was "happy in the hull," meaning she was not in charge of the Bears' operation, and George McCaskey scoffed.

"Happy in the hull? Are you kidding?" George said. "She's in the prow. She's got the night watch. She's looking for icebergs. With her at the helm, the seas are calmer, the storms less severe. She's the guiding force behind the Bears, and everybody at Halas Hall—including the players—knows that and appreciates that. That's why the goal of everybody here is to see her holding the Super Bowl trophy."

George first worked for the Bears as an office assistant at the age of 14, and served as a ball boy for Bears training camps. He became ticket manager in 1991, and worked in the ticket office for 20 years before being tabbed as chairman of the board.

68 Bears as Actors

It might be fair to say the Chicago Bears are the most lovable of all NFL teams. Although their one logo shows a growling Bear, they have always been a family-friendly team, perhaps because they are still owned by a family, the McCaskeys, who are direct descendants of Bears owner and founder George Halas.

Either way, the Bears have always been appreciated by modern American culture.

The first Chicago Bear to turn his playing career into a TV and movie career might have been former linebacker Dick Butkus. Constantly portraying a gruff, burly character, Butkus made a name for himself originally by appearing in a very funny series of Miller Lite commercials that ran for years. He turned that popularity into a longtime career and appeared in over 30 TV series, sometimes with a continuing character. He had recurring supporting roles on the TV shows *My Two Dads* and *Hang Time.*

He also appeared in 10 movies over his career.

The 1985 Super Bowl team, headed by popular, mouthy, funny, and irreverent head coach Mike Ditka, probably started that love affair. When the team created "The Super Bowl Shuffle" video, and did so *before* winning the Super Bowl, they stepped over and ahead of most other NFL teams in terms of popularity.

Many TV shows that were based in Chicago made no bones about their appreciation of the Bears. Characters regularly wore Bears jerseys on the show, especially on programs like *Married... with Children* and *According to Jim,* which starred famous Bears fan Jim Belushi, brother of even more famous Bears fan John Belushi.

The popularity of that Bears team turned many players into stars, and they carried that stardom into TV and movies.

Mike Ditka often portrayed himself in TV and movies, and his most famous role came in the 2005 film *Kicking and Screaming,* in which he argued and berated famed actor Robert Duvall, who was a neighbor in the film. He played himself on numerous TV shows, including *Coach.* He appeared as himself twice on *Saturday Night Live,* which loved to reference the Chicago Bears because so many of the show's regular comedic actors came from or trained in Chicago.

Walter Payton, the most popular Bear of all time, had the cherub face and bubbling personality to make him a no-brainer for TV. He co-hosted *Saturday Night Live* with former San Francisco

49ers quarterback Joe Montana in 1987, and also played himself on *Coach.*

Willie Gault, the flashy good-looking wide receiver, went hard after the acting career, and appeared in numerous TV shows and movies. He was a regular contributor to the popular political program *The West Wing* in the early 2000s.

William "the Refrigerator" Perry was not an actor, but that did not stop dozens of TV shows from using him to portray himself in key cameo appearances. One of his most famous roles was as himself on the 1980s action show *The A-Team.* He was often called on to appear as himself in TV movies, to give the show a genuine Chicago feel.

Bears quarterback Jim McMahon took a turn at acting, and had two TV appearances and one movie appearance where he did not play himself. They were one-time deals. He portrayed himself in the film *Johnny Dangerously* and on the popular TV show *The League.*

Defensive end Otis Wilson twice appeared in films in minor roles. He was a jail officer in the Chicago-based film *The Fugitive* starring Harrison Ford and Tommy Lee Jones.

And if you consider professional wrestling acting, Perry and Steve McMichael were regular performers for the WWF (now the WWE) in the 1980s. McMichael continued that career path with the World Championship Wrestling (WCW) organization through the 1990s.

69 Saying Goodbye to Payton

Walter Payton died too early. In 1999, at the age of 45, he died from complications relating to the autoimmune liver disease that caused him to suffer from bile duct cancer. The city and the NFL mourned him for a long time thereafter.

Every NFL team held special ceremonies to honor Payton upon his death. The Bears wore No. 34 patches on their jerseys to remember him.

A public memorial service was held at Soldier Field, where Payton toiled for the Bears for his entire 13-year career. Payton's wife, Connie, and his children, Jarrett and Brittney, all spoke before the estimated crowd of 15,000. So did NFL commissioner Paul Tagliabue. Chosen to represent his teammates was defensive lineman Dan Hampton.

"I thank the city of Chicago for loving Walter as much as my family and I did," Connie Payton said at the ceremony.

Numerous cancer-related organizations were born out of Payton's untimely passing. The Walter and Connie Payton Foundation still does work in the areas of organ donation. The Walter Payton Liver Center is now operating at the University of Illinois at Chicago Medical Center, where Payton received treatment.

In 2007, the city of Chicago named a high school after him. The Walter Payton College Preparatory High School is one of the most prestigious high schools in the city.

Payton died 12 years after he finished playing, but his spirit was infused in the team, for whom he continued to cheer and stay in contact with.

Walter Payton/Michael Jordan

Walter Payton played for the Chicago Bears from 1975 to 1987. Michael Jordan played for the Chicago Bulls from 1984 to 1993, took a two-year break, then played for them again until 1998.

So Chicago enjoyed the talents of two of the most iconic athletes in two different sports at the same time for four years, from 1984 to 1987. If you want to start a spirited argument in a sports bar, gather the patrons and ask which athlete means more to the city of Chicago, Payton or Jordan?

Jordan and Payton did occasionally interact, although not for public purposes. There was never any attempt by either to compare himself to the other. Payton was at the end of a Hall of Fame career. Jordan was at the beginning. But for sports fans, it was a heck of a time to live in and cheer for Chicago.

Payton's untimely death in 1999 came at a time when Jordan was moving into his second retirement. Jordan felt Payton's passing just as so many other fans and Chicago residents did. He issued a statement at the time of Payton's death.

"Walter was a Chicago icon long before I arrived there," Jordan said. "He was a great man off the field, and his on-the-field accomplishments speak for themselves. I spent a lot of time with Walter, and I truly feel that we have lost a great man."

On November 7, 1999, a bad Chicago Bears team went to Green Bay to play the Packers. The Packers would finish 8–8 that season but at the time of the game they were still in the hunt for the NFC Central Division title. The Bears, and Payton, helped push back those plans. The Bears had not beaten the Packers since 1993 in one of the longest-running dominant periods for either team in that historic series.

The night before the game, Bears defensive coordinator Greg Blache referenced Payton in a speech to the team. The Bears, on their way to a 6–10 record, appeared to play their hearts out before a hostile crowd.

In a low-scoring game, the Packers lined up to kick a game-winning 28-yard field goal, which in most cases is a sure thing in the NFL. Packers placekicker Ryan Longwell, one of the more dependable kickers in the league, lined up the attempt, but Bears defensive end Bryan Robinson reached up from his 6'4" frame and blocked the kick, preserving the victory.

"I think Walter Payton actually picked me up a little bit and boosted me up in the air because I can't jump that high," Robinson said after the game. "Walter had a lot to do with it. I know he did."

70 When the Bears Drafted in the Top Five

The NFL draft started in 1936 and operated as a way for weak or poor-performing teams to get better while fairly staffing player rosters with the best collegiate players available. The teams with the worst records had the right to the top picks, which they could use to select a college player or trade to a better team in order to acquire more picks farther down in the draft.

The rules surrounding the NFL draft have changed over the years, but by the 21st century it had become a dazzling spectacle for informed college and NFL football fans. Writers and broadcasters created mock drafts, trying to guess how the players would be selected, and often the mock drafts started the minute the previous NFL season ended and draft position was set. Fans gathered wherever the draft took place to cheer or boo their favorite team's selections. The NFL began moving the site of its central draft headquarters to various NFL cities to spread the excitement surrounding the event.

Fans of all 32 NFL teams waited with bated breath to see how their team would use their available draft picks, but nothing riled up a fan base more than when their favored team had a top five pick in the first round. Very often, those fans had seen their team muddle through a disastrous season, thus earning one of the top picks. The draft slot became a reward for long-suffering fans as well as for the team itself.

In the Bears' long history, they had a top five pick 18 times. Expansion made it more difficult to acquire top five picks as the years went on, and in the Super Bowl era, the Bears had only seven through the 2020 season.

Here are the details of each of those key selections over the years:

1939—Sid Luckman, quarterback out of Columbia, was selected second overall. He is the topic of Chapter 6 of this book, so that worked out.

1941—Tom Harmon, Heisman Trophy–winning halfback out of Michigan, was the No. 1 pick in the draft. He never signed with the Bears. After graduation, he was drafted into the Air Force. Two years later, he played two seasons for the L.A. Rams.

1941—Norm Standlee, fullback from Stanford, was the No. 3 player selected.

1946—Johnny Lujack, quarterback from Notre Dame, was the No. 4 pick of the draft, and is widely considered the third best quarterback in Bears history. His take is in Chapter 33 of this book.

1947—Bob Fenimore, halfback out of Oklahoma Stare. Only the second No. 1 pick in the draft for the Bears,

1948—Bobby Layne, quarterback out of Texas, was the third pick in the draft. Luckman and Lujack were already on the team at that time, and team owner George Hakas Had created the greatest three-headed Quarterback Club in NFL history. See Chapter 92 for more information.

1950—Chuck Hunsinger, halfback out of Florida, was the No. 3 player in the draft.

1951—Bob Williams, quarterback from Notre Dame, was the No. 2 pick.

1961—Mike Ditka, tight end from the University of Pittsburgh, was the No. 5 pick in the draft, and became one of the most consequential No. 5 picks in NFL history. His story can be read in Chapter 4 (when he was Bears coach) and Chapter 23 (when he invented the tight end position in the NFL as a player).

1965—Dick Butkus, linebacker from Illinois, and halfback Gale Sayers from Kansas, we're the No. 3 and No. 4 picks in the draft that year. This is considered the greatest draft year in Bears history. Details on their careers can be read in Chapters 17 (Butkus) and 32 (Sayers).

1972—Lionel Antoine, offensive tackle from Southern Illinois, was the No. 3 pick.

1974—Waymond Bryant, a linebacker from Tennessee State, was the No. 4 pick in the draft.

1975—Walter Payton, a halfback from Jackson State, was the No. 4 pick that year. Selected ahead of him were California quarterback Steve Bartkowski, Hall of Fame defensive tackle Randy White out of Maryland, and guard Ken Huff from North Carolina. More on Payton can be read in multiple chapters of this book.

1979—Dan Hampton, a defensive tackle from Arkansas, was the No. 4 pick. You can read more about Hampton in Chapter 99.

1982—Jim McMahon, a quarterback from Brigham Young, was the No. 5 pick. His story is in Chapter 27.

1998—Curtis Enis, a running back out of Penn State, was the No. 5 pick.

2005—Cedric Benson, a running back from the University of Texas, was the No. 4 pick.

2017—Mitchell Trubisky, a quarterback out of the University of North Carolina, was the No. 2 pick.

With the verdict still out on Trubisky in 2020, it is fair to say the Bears were very successful with at least eight of their top 5 picks. Do you agree?

71 Bulldog Turner

In 1940, the Chicago Bears used their first-round draft pick to select a two-way player out of Hardin-Simmons College in Abilene, Texas, named Clyde Turner. He played 13 years for the Bears as a center and linebacker.

He started both ways for the 1940 team, his first, and had an interception and fumble recovery in the Bears' 73–0 title game win over the Washington Redskins, the most dominant victory in NFL history. In 1942, he set a team record with eight interceptions. The Bears won four championships with Turner at the "center" spot on both sides of the ball.

He finished his career with 17 interceptions and two touchdowns, including a 96-yard run against the Washington Redskins in 1947. In that game, the Redskins quarterback was Hall of Famer Sammy Baugh, who went to the same high school as Turner and was a teammate for two years. When Turner went for the long touchdown run, the last few yards he carried Baugh on his back as Baugh tried to stop him from scoring.

Turner also had a fumble recovery for a touchdown in his career.

Turner was an amazing athlete who almost didn't get selected by the Bears, or anybody, because he played at tiny Hardin-Simmons.

Clyde "Bulldog" Turner at Bears training camp in 1946.

College scouting at the time concentrated on the bigger schools; the only two NFL teams that knew about him at all were the Bears and the Detroit Lions. The Lions had promised Turner they would draft him, and had every intention of grabbing him in the second round. But the Bears knew about the Lions' interest, and after reading a scout's lengthy description of Turner, George Halas made him the Bears' first-round pick.

The Bears were using the newfangled T-formation in the 1940s, and Turner's ability as a center made him valuable and made the new system work. He was known on offense for his ability to snap the ball with precision, and his ability to get out on the block for sweeping runs.

On defense, Turner was a ballhawk and ferocious hitter, which perpetuated his "Bulldog" nickname.

He was unusually quick for a lineman, and when the Bears needed a player to run the ball in a game in 1944 (their running back had been ejected from the game for fighting), he scored a touchdown on his only carry, going 48 yards for the score. He may have been the only center to ever be used as a punt and kickoff returner as well.

The Bears went to the NFL Championship Game each of Turner's first four years in the league. In 1945, Turner was called into military service and played in only two games. He returned to the Bears in 1946 and the Bears won the title again that season.

As a player, Turner was known for the fact that he could, if asked to do so, play every position on the field. He studied the team on both sides of the ball, and knew everyone's responsibilities on every play. When he retired as a player in 1952, it was obvious that he would become a coach.

Turner worked for the Bears for four years, then went to work at Baylor University in his home state of Texas. When the new American Football League, a rival for the NFL, was created in 1960, Sammy Baugh was named coach of the New York Titans and he recruited Turner to serve as an assistant. Eventually, Baugh got fired from the head coaching job and it was given to Turner, who coached the Titans for only one season, 1962.

He was elected into the Pro Football Hall of Fame in 1966.

72 Bill Swerski's Superfans

Stereotypes can be funny, when shown with the proper amount of respect. Or sometimes, when the stereotypes are taken to a ridiculous extreme, they can be less hurtful and more hilarious.

The stereotype of a Chicago Bears fan as a beer-drinking, cigar-smoking, often-belching, heart-attack-waiting-to-happen kind of guy became the basis for one of the longest-running skits in the history of *Saturday Night Live.*

The skit, which became known as "The Superfans," came from the mind of comedy writer Robert Smigel, who had paid his comic dues as a skit writer and performer in Chicago in the 1980s. He was hired to write for *SNL* in 1985, but when a writers' strike kept him off that job, he worked with a Chicago comedy troupe and created the Superfans. When the writers' strike ended, he gave the Superfans to *SNL.*

The first appearance of the Superfans on *SNL* was in 1991, and included talented Chicago movie-and-TV actor Joe Mantegna along with Smigel and *SNL* regulars Chris Farley and Mike Myers. They all wore Bears gear, had moustaches similar to that of famed Bears coach Mike Ditka, and smoked cigars. Whenever the Bears came up in conversation, they would say in unison "Da Bears" in a sing-song style that became legendary.

Mantegna was not a regular on *SNL,* so his character was replaced by actor George Wendt, another Chicago-trained comedy actor who was famous for his role as George on the Boston-based bar series *Cheers.* John Goodman, another famous TV-and-movie actor, would appear in the skit when he appeared as host of *SNL.*

The humor in the skit usually came from the group's love of both the Chicago Bears and Mike Ditka. They would predict the outcome of upcoming Bears games, always selecting the Bears. They eventually got around to predicting the outcome of numerous other sporting events that would involve Ditka, including Ditka versus a hurricane, with Ditka the easy winner. They then had to decide who would win between Ditka and a hurricane named Ditka.

Another source of humor in the skits was the constant string of heart attacks the members suffered as a result of their Polish sausage and beer lifestyle and getting worked up during arguments. Whenever a member was absent (because the actor was unavailable) his absence was explained as a medical emergency resulting from heart trouble.

When the Chicago Bulls started wining championships behind Michael Jordan in the early 1990s, the Superfans added that NBA team to their allegiance, declaring "Da Bulls" as the best team in the NBA. They once were asked to argue "Da Bears" against "Da Bulls" in one of their later skits, but explained that the contest would result in a tear in the space-time continuum, and therefore had to be stopped by the United Nations.

The Superfans showed the national interest the 1985 Super Bowl Bears produced, as well as the 1990s Chicago Bulls. But they did add the annoying "Da Bears" and "Da Bulls" sayings to the Chicago lexicon. They have not yet apologized for that.

73 Spare Bears

The 1987 NFL season was the most unusual one of all time. A strike by the NFL players over the Collective Bargaining Agreement put a temporary halt to the season after the second game, and the players stayed away for four weeks.

But the NFL did not halt play. Instead, they hired replacement players to play for the league's teams. One week of games was cancelled to prepare these replacements, but the league did play three games with the new players before order was restored.

In American labor parlance, a person who replaces a laborer who is on strike is known as a "scab," a particularly mean name given to someone who steps past the picket lines and goes to work. All other NFL teams had "scabs," but the Bears' group of replacement players came to be known as the "Spare Bears."

The 1987 regular Bears still had a number of holdovers from the 1985 Super Bowl team. The 1986 season had been a disappointment because the Bears did not repeat. Jim McMahon was still around after his injury-plagued previous season, and the Bears had drafted a quarterback to serve as McMahon's eventual replacement. That quarterback was Jim Harbaugh, who would one day coach the San Francisco 49ers.

Walter Payton was also still on the team, but 1987 would be his last season.

All NFL teams had to go out and dig up players to serve as replacements, and the Bears found a local hero to serve as a quarterback. Sean Payton, who had been a quarterback at Naperville High School outside of Chicago and Eastern Illinois to the south, had been playing indoor football when the Bears found him. Payton, who eventually became the coach of the New Orleans Saints and won Super Bowl XLIV, was horrible as a passing quarterback with only eight completions on 23 attempts in three games.

The Spare Bears won their first game against the Eagles 35–3 in front of only 4,000 fans in Philadelphia. NFL faithful were none too pleased with the league or the players for the strike and chose not to show up for what were deemed "fake" NFL games, even though the results would stand.

With several members of the real Bears walking a picket line in front of Soldier Field, 32,000 fans showed up on October 11 to watch the Spare Bears beat the Minnesota Vikings 27–7, making the Bears 4–0. Then a crowd of almost 47,000 showed up at Soldier Field the next week to see the Spare Bears lose to the New Orleans Saints 19–17.

The real Bears were 2–0 when the strike happened, and the Spare Bears were 2–1 in their short time together. The strike ended in mid-October and the NFL completed 15 of their scheduled 16 games. The Bears finished 11–4 that year and made the playoffs, once again raising hopes that they could reach another Super Bowl. Instead, they lost their playoff game to the Washington Redskins.

Ditka had been pro-management through the entire strike, and referred to the Spare Bears as his "real" team. When the strike was over, he gave the Bears the chance to vote whether to allow any of the Spare Bears to remain with the team. The team voted overwhelmingly not to allow that to happen, and Ditka didn't care. He did maintain several players from the Spare Bear roster, including tight end Glen Kozlowski, who had been drafted by the Bears, crossed the picket line to play, and ended up staying with the team for six years.

Another person who started a career as a result of being a Spare Bear was quarterback Mike Hohensee. He was undrafted out of the University of Minnesota, and played in the upstart United States

Football League and the Canadian Football League before joining the Bears.

Once the strike ended, he again played in the Arena Football League, then became a coach, and in 2001 he became head coach of the new Chicago Rush of the Arena Football League. He coached the Rush for eight seasons initially, won an Arena Bowl title, and then came back to coach the Rush again in 2010.

74 Coaches Between Halas and Ditka

Eventually, George Halas figured out it was time to quit coaching.

Halas coached the Bears from 1920—when the team was still the Decatur Staleys—to 1967, but he took three breaks from the sideline job during those years. From 1929 to 1933, he served in World War I. From 1942 to 1946, he served again during World War II. In 1956, he turned the team over to his longtime friend Paddy Driscoll, but he couldn't stay away.

Finally, in 1967, he stopped coached. But he was still the owner, and still very involved with the daily operations. It was up to him who would coach the team.

Following the 1981 season, he went over the head of his first general manager, Jim Finks, and hired Dallas Cowboys assistant coach and former Bears tight end Mike Ditka to coach the team. That was definitely one hire he got correct.

But the four coaches he had between 1967 and 1982 weren't so strong.

Jim Dooley, who coached the Bears from 1968 to 1971, was a former Bears player, joining the team in 1952. He played on both sides of the ball, but made a name for himself as a wide receiver, scoring 11 touchdowns in his second and third seasons. He missed almost two full seasons to serve in the Air Force, but came back to play for the Bears through the 1961 season.

In his seven-plus seasons he caught 211 passes and scored 16 touchdowns.

Upon retirement, Dooley immediately became a part of Halas' coaching staff, working with the defensive backs. When Halas and defensive coordinator George Allen had their falling out, Dooley moved into Allen's role. While serving as defensive coordinator, he initiated a defensive scheme that would place five defensive backs into the lineup on obvious passing downs. It was the first time a defense went all out to defend against the pass, and the defense became known as the nickel (for "five") defense.

In May of 1968, Halas stepped down as coach due to struggles with arthritis. He immediately named Dooley his successor.

In 1968, the Dooley-led Bears went 7–7, then in 1969 they suffered the worst season in Bears' history, going 1–13. No Bears team had ever won less than three games prior to that. The Bears went 6–8 in both 1970 and 1971, and Halas fired Dooley after the 1971 season. He finished with a record of 20–36 and had no playoff appearances.

The Bears list Dooley as the first coach in team history ever to be fired. The others weren't fired; they were usurped by Halas when he returned to the sidelines.

For a new coach, Halas was not going to consider someone who did not have some connection to the Bears. Abe Gibron, who had played two seasons at offensive guard for the Bears, was the team's offensive line coach for seven years, with some time under Halas and some under Dooley. Halas tabbed Gibron to be his new coach.

Gibron was a huge man. He was large as a player and didn't get any smaller when he stopped playing. But he also had a large personality and was relatively happy-go-lucky as football coaches go.

None of that helped him when it came to coaching the Bears, who were going through their longest dry spell in terms of championships—or even championship game appearances. Not since 1963's title had the Bears even been to the playoffs when Gibron took over in 1972. The Bears were transitioning from the Gale Sayers–Dick Butkus Bears to a starless team, and Gibron paid the price. In three years, the Bears were 11–30–1 and again had no playoff appearances when Gibron was fired at the end of the 1974 season.

(Gibron, by the way, can be seen playing himself in the made-for-TV movie *Brian's Song*.)

By 1975, Halas had turned over some team operations to his son, George Jr. (known as "Mugs"). Mugs convinced his dad to let him hire a general manager, and the Bears grabbed talented front-office man Jim Finks from Minnesota. It was Finks who decided the Bears should hire former star linebacker Jack Pardee as coach.

Pardee was 39 years old when he came to the Bears after coaching one season in the upstart World Football League (WFL). He was the youngest coach in the league at the time. After going 4–10 in his first season, the Bears were 7–7 in 1976 and Pardee was named NFC Coach of the Year. In 1977, Pardee coaxed a 9–5 record out of the team, which was good enough to get them in the playoff, but they were severely outclassed by the Dallas Cowboys 37–7.

But Pardee was frustrated with the state of the Bears at the time. They did not have their own practice facility, and were moving between the University of Chicago and Lake Forest College to find a place to work out. At those locations, they either had no locker room or were using the women's locker room at

Lake Forest. They had to schedule their practices around the school's teams' needs.

The Washington Redskins, for whom Pardee had ended his playing career as a linebacker, came calling, and Pardee left the Bears at the end of his contract to become coach of the Redskins. Pardee finished his time with the Bears with a record of 20–22, but he did make it to the postseason.

After eight seasons as a defensive coach with the Minnesota Vikings, Neill Armstrong was hired to be the next coach of the Bears. A favorite of Bears general manager Jim Finks from Finks' time with the Vikings, Armstrong had played both wide receiver and defensive back in the league, as well as having spent six years as the head coach of the Edmonton Eskimos of the Canadian Football League.

As a member of the Minnesota's coaching staff, he was part of a defense that helped the Vikings get to the playoffs seven times in the eight years he was with the club. In three of those seasons, the Vikings got to the Super Bowl, but lost all three times. Still, they got there, something the Bears had not yet done in the short history of the Super Bowl.

In his four seasons, the Bears had one winning campaign, when they went 10–6 in 1979, and they lost their playoff game to the Philadelphia Eagles 27–17. At that point the Bears were 16 years removed from their last championship. After two sub-.500 seasons, Armstrong was fired, and Halas Sr. made his last major decision, to hire Ditka from the Cowboys and bring him back to the Bears fold.

The rest, as they say, is history.

75 The Fog Bowl

Weather is a huge part of being a Chicago Bears fan. Cold weather combined with wind plays a part not only in the way the game is played, but also in the way a fan has to dress to watch the Bears play at Soldier Field, or at Wrigley Field before that (unless you want to show that you have painted one of the letters in the word "Bears" on your chest).

But fog? That's a different animal.

Fog, from a technical standpoint, is a cloud of tiny ice droplets that aren't exactly affected by gravity the way rain is. Fog just sort of hangs around like a cloud.

On December 31, 1988, at a time of year when the Bears usually have to worry about snow and ice when they host a game, the weather factor instead was fog—heavy, dense, nearly impenetrable fog.

That day the Bears, coached by Mike Ditka, were hosting the Philadelphia Eagles, coached by former Bears defensive coordinator and Ditka-rival Buddy Ryan, in an NFC divisional playoff game. The Bears had gone 12–4 that season and had home-field advantage over the 10–6 Eagles.

At one point during the second quarter, the fog rolled in from the lake to the east, and soon it blanketed the entire playing surface. Visibility dropped to a point where no one could see where they were in relation to the sideline. Forward passes were impossible because quarterbacks could not see receivers and receivers could not see the approaching ball, even if it was thrown in their direction.

McMahon and Ditka pass without a word during the Fog Bowl. (Courtesy of Getty Images)

Broadcasters could not see the field at all. Philadelphia quarterback Randall Cunningham admitted that his 65-yard pass to tight end Keith Jackson was a guess.

NFL officials went to both Ditka and Ryan to ask how they felt about continuing the game. Neither coach asked for a delay or stoppage of play. They came from the same school of football, that nothing would stop a game, certainly nothing as relatively inoffensive as a deep fog.

"If this was a baseball game, maybe," Ryan said. "But this is football, and you have to play the game."

The 65,000 fans in attendance had no idea what was going on. The television audience had to watch a view from field level, because cameras above ground were ineffective. The broadcasters watched the field-level telecast and called the game that way. A suggestion to move a broadcaster to the field was nixed because it was determined he wouldn't be able to see anything anyway.

The Bears beat the Eagles 20–12, and timing had something to do with it. They scored two touchdowns in the first half before the thickest part of the fog rolled in.

Although it wasn't a bowl game of any sort, the game was immediately tagged as the "Fog Bowl." It's considered one of the worst weather-condition games in the history of the NFL.

The Bears then went on to play the San Francisco 49ers in the NFC Championship Game the next week for a chance to return once again to the Super Bowl, but they lost that game 28–3.

76 1983 NFL Draft

Fans of the Chicago Bears' 1985 Super Bowl team can name the starters on each side of the ball. Twenty-two names, and every one of them is etched in the memory of Bears fans who witnessed the greatest team win the most dominant Super Bowl in NFL history.

But what is not known as well is how the players came to the Bears. The answer, for many of them, is that they were drafted in 1983.

The 1983 NFL Draft day for the Chicago Bears is considered one of the best in league history. Jim Finks, the Hall of Fame executive who had been the first general manager in Bears history, was in charge of the 1983 draft, even though he was prepared to resign the day the draft was over because team owner George Halas had gone over his head to sign the new coach, Mike Ditka, the year before. But Finks stayed around to handle the draft, which may have helped put him in the Hall of Fame.

Here are the players selected in that draft who contributed to the 1985 Super Bowl team:

Jim Covert—the offensive tackle out of Pittsburgh was the sixth pick of the first round. Jimbo was an immediate starter and was an All-Pro four years in a row.

Willie Gault—the Bears had a second pick in the first round from a former deal with the Tampa Bay Buccaneers and used it to draft the wide receiver out of Tennessee. Gault, who was also a member of a world-record setting 4x100 meter relay team, ended up scoring 45 touchdowns in an 11-year career, and was the long-range speed threat the Bears needed to open up the field for Walter Payton coming out of the backfield.

Mike Richardson—with the fifth pick of the second round, the Bears grabbed the defensive back out of Arizona State. He had 20 picks and one touchdown in six seasons with the Bears, and was one of the starting cornerbacks for the Super Bowl team.

Dave Duerson—the Bears picked eighth in the third round and amazingly got another starting defensive back out of the deal, this one from Notre Dame. In his career, Duerson had 20 interceptions and an unusually large number of sacks for a safety with 16.

Tom Thayer—picking seventh in the fourth round, the Bears again went to Notre Dame and grabbed yet another offensive lineman. Thayer played guard for the Super Bowl Bears, and after his playing career was over he became a key member of the Bears' radio broadcast team.

Richard Dent—all the way down in the eighth round, the Bears found one of their best players ever, the one that became the Most Valuable Player of Super Bowl XX. Dent, who played collegiately at Tennessee State, had 17 sacks in the 1985 season, and in the Super Bowl he shared two sacks and forced two fumbles.

Mark Bortz—later in the eighth round the Bears found the third member of the starting offensive line for the Super Bowl team when they tabbed a guard out of the University of Iowa. Bortz played for the Bears for 12 seasons.

The 1983 NFL Draft was also notable for having three Hall of Fame quarterbacks selected in the first round: John Elway, Dan Marino, and Jim Kelly. The Bears instead concentrated on the players to protect their quarterback, Jim McMahon, and it worked out to the tune of the team's only Super Bowl victory.

77 Doug Atkins

When people tell stories about George Halas, they love to talk about the testy but respectful relationship he had with two leaders from the Green Bay Packers, Curly Lambeau and Vince Lombardi.

But Halas had another difficult relationship during his coaching career, and this one came from within.

Doug Atkins, the giant of a man who played for the Bears for 12 seasons, loved to test Halas, and would frequently call him late at night to berate him about his contract, about the state of the team, about whatever came to his mind. Halas would always tell Atkins to sober up and they would talk in the morning.

Atkins was a 6'8" monster who played defensive end. He was very difficult to pass over, because of his height and the fact that he was agile enough to compete in the high jump in high school and win the SEC title in that competition while at Tennessee.

That leaping skill served him when he was going forward as well. He liked to jump over offensive linemen as they approached him for a block. Since they had their head down to try to get the huge man down, it was easy for Atkins to leap over them and get to the quarterback.

Atkins was drafted by the Cleveland Browns in 1953, and won the NFL title with the Browns in 1954. But the Bears were able to trade for him for the 1955 season, and he helped anchor the defense that won the NFL title in 1963. Atkins was one of the most popular players on what was the most popular team in Chicago history until the Super Bowl team of 1985.

Atkins came from Tennessee. Although he was known for his angry style of play on the field, he was far less intense when he wasn't in a game. He was often criticized for not putting in a full effort in practice, and it was Halas who had to find a way to deal with him. But Halas kept Atkins on the team for 12 years, so something must have worked well between them.

Atkins played in an era before sacks were a regularly kept statistic, so there are no numbers to determine just how many times he got to the quarterback. But he remains one of the most dangerous defensive ends in NFL history, and Halas himself said he was the best defensive end in the history of the game.

Off the field, Atkins was a character. He liked to drink, and he liked to show off his array of weapons. He would show up at training camp with a selection of firearms. He would drink to his fill, and then dial up Halas for one of those late-night conversations.

After the 1966 season, Halas and Atkins had yet another conversation about Atkins' contract. Eventually, the conversation turned into a disagreement and Halas traded Atkins to the New Orleans Saints at the age of 37.

Atkins was elected to the Pro Football Hall of Fame in 1982.

78 Richard Dent

So why was Richard Dent still available in the eighth round of the 1983 NFL Draft?

The 6'5" defensive end played football at Tennessee State University, not a hotbed of pro football talent at the time. The Bears made the selection of Dent (203rd overall that year) and found the final piece of the puzzle to the most dominating defense in NFL history.

In his rookie season under head coach Mike Ditka, Dent only had three sacks, but after that he sent fear into offensive lines with his athletic abilities. In 1984, he had 17.5 sacks and in 1985 he had a league-leading 17 sacks, with an interception for a touchdown to go with them. In those two years, he also forced 11 fumbles, recovered three fumbles, and had 77 tackles as well.

In the NFC divisional playoff game against the New York Giants in 1985, Dent had 3.5 sacks, seven tackles, and forced two fumbles. The Bears won that game by shutting out the Giants.

Future Hall of Famers Richard Dent and Joe Montana enjoy a more civilized interaction than usual during practices before an exhibition in Berlin in 1991.

Dent had another sack in the NFC title game against the Rams, another shutout.

In the Super Bowl, Dent shared two sacks, forced a pair of fumbles, and blocked a pass. He was named the MVP of Super Bowl XX, and became only the fifth defensive player in 20 years to be named MVP of the season's final game.

Dent was so good at his craft not because he was meaner or bigger than any other player at his position. What made him so good as a defensive end was that he was unbelievably quick for his size, and he was relentless. He battled to get past his blocker and get to the passer until he knew the play was over. Once he got to the passer, his ability to wrap the man up and put him down helped him add up his sacks.

Thanks to his appearance and solo singing effort in "The Super Bowl Shuffle," the Bears' braggadocio pre–Super Bowl video, Dent became known as "the Sackman."

In his 12-year career with the Bears, he had 124.5 sacks, eight interceptions, 641 tackles, and 13 fumble recoveries. Those are Hall of Fame–worthy numbers, but it took Dent several years to finally get the nod in 2011.

After leaving the Bears following the 1993 season, Dent became very vocal about his displeasure with the way Mike Ditka handled the team following the 1985 Super Bowl, placing the blame for the Bears failing to return to the championship game squarely on the shoulders of his former coach. He was especially critical of the fact that Ditka brought in diminutive quarterback Doug Flutie to replace injured quarterback Jim McMahon in 1986 when Dent thought the other backups, Steve Fuller and Mike Tomczak, could have pulled the Bears through the playoffs and into the title game themselves. After going 14–2 in the regular season, the Bears lost a home game to the Washington Redskins 27–13 with Flutie at the helm of the offense.

Dent played for the San Francisco 49ers and Philadelphia Eagles after he left the Bears.

When he finally made it into the Hall of Fame after seven nominations, Dent did not acknowledge Ditka, or his defensive coordinator at the time, Buddy Ryan.

79 Offensive Linemen in the Hall of Fame

It's hard to get into the Pro Football Hall of Fame. It's especially hard to get in as an offensive lineman.

What statistic do you put down when you want to nominate an offensive lineman for the Hall of Fame? There isn't one. Reputation from playing on the offensive line comes from holding your own against the strongest and fastest players on the other team to protect your quarterback or being able to run out from a three-point stance to provide a key block for your running back.

There aren't numbers that represent success at any of those skills.

Of the league-leading 30 people who are in the Pro Football Hall of Fame and played or worked the majority of their careers with the Bears, 11 of them are offensive linemen. That's a huge number of players who have been congratulated and rewarded for their hard work in the trenches.

Working from the first to be inducted to the last, the Chicago Bears' offensive linemen in the Hall of Fame are:

George Trafton—Trafton was a member of the very first Chicago Bears team, back when it was known as the Decatur Staleys. He was a center, and history tells us he was the first center to snap the ball with one hand, allowing for a better ability to deal with onrushing defenders with the other. Trafton was a native Chicagoan, having grown up in south-suburban Oak Park. He also attended the University of Notre Dame.

George Connor—the question about Connor is whether to count him as an offensive tackle, a defensive tackle, or a linebacker. He did all three well enough to get into the Hall of Fame. He was recognized as an All-NFL player at each of those positions during his career.

Dan Fortmann—Fortmann was a ninth-round draft pick out of Colgate for the Bears in 1936. He played eight seasons for the Bears, during which the team won three titles.

Ed Healey—another member of one of the first Bears teams, Healey played for the Orange and Blue from 1922 to 1927. Healey played offensive tackle and was named an All-Pro four times in his career.

Bill Hewitt—Hewitt played for the Bears from 1932 to 1936 and played on the line on both sides of the ball. He is considered the last holdout of those players who refused to wear a helmet, stubbornly avoiding it until the last year of his career.

Stan Jones—Jones was named the nation's most outstanding lineman in 1953 after his collegiate career at the University of Maryland. With the Bears he was named to the Pro Bowl seven times, and he was on the 1963 NFL championship team. He started with the Bears as an offensive tackle but switched to guard early in his pro career. He switched to the defensive side of the ball late in his career with the Bears.

Link Lyman—Lyman played for the Bears from 1926 to 1934 and was part of the barnstorming tour with Red Grange in his first year with the team. He won four NFL titles with three different teams.

George Musso—Musso played for the Bears from 1933 to 1944 and moved from tackle to guard, earning All-Pro designations at both positions. He played in seven championship games for the Bears during that time and won four of them.

Joe Stydahar—Stydahar is known for playing without a helmet early in his career. He played for the Bears twice, from 1936 to 1942 and again in 1945 and 1946. He was named All-NFL five straight seasons.

Clyde "Bulldog" Turner—Turner played both center on offense and linebacker on defense. Although he was named All-Pro six times as a center, he also led the league in interceptions in 1942 with eight.

Patrick Mannelly

What is the most underappreciated position on a football team? You might think punter or placekicker, or you might say center, but you would be wrong.

The most underappreciated position on a football team is the long snapper, which is indeed a center, but it is a center with a specific duty. The long snapper is responsible for hiking the ball 13 to 15 yards back to a punter or seven to eight yards back to the holder for place kicks. When done correctly, it is hardly ever noticed, but being able to do it correctly is a specific skill set.

In 2012, Patrick Mannelly completed his 15th season as the Bears' primary long snapper, and that made him the player with the longest tenure in a Bears uniform ever. None of the great names in Bears history, including Walter Payton (13 seasons), Dick Butkus (nine seasons), Sid Luckman (12 seasons), Brian Urlacher (13 seasons), or George Halas himself (10 seasons) managed to play 15 seasons with the Bears.

Mannelly also signed a contract to play for the Bears in 2013, which would extend his team-record tenure. That tenure includes the record for most games played as a Bear, which was 231 at the end of the 2012 season.

Mannelly was drafted by the Bears in the sixth round of the 1998 draft. He played collegiately at Duke University.

Jimbo Covert—Played tackle for the Super Bowl–champion Bears. He was a graduate of the University of Pittsburgh, which made him a favorite of coach Ditka.

So there you have it. The best Chicago Bears of the least acknowledged players in the NFL, offensive linemen.

80 George McAfee

George McAfee was already famous when he came to the Bears. His performance as a running back at Duke University was good enough to eventually put him in the College Football Hall of Fame. In 1939, he led the Blue Devils as a rusher, a receiver, and a scorer. He was the team's primary kick returner, punt returner, led the team in interceptions on defense, and also punted. He led Duke to an appearance in the Rose Bowl on the other coast in 1938.

Like Halas and many other players at the time, McAfee was also talented on the baseball diamond. He was the team's center fielder at Duke and batted .353 as a senior before being drafted into the NFL. Oh, yeah, he also won Duke's conference 100-meter title in the spring of 1939.

McAfee was drafted out of Duke with the second-overall pick in the draft by the Philadelphia Eagles, who turned around and immediately traded him to the Bears for three offensive linemen. He played eight seasons for the Bears, although he spent three years in the Navy during World War II when he might have made even more impact in the NFL.

In his first regular season game, he returned a kickoff 93 yards for a touchdown and also threw a touchdown pass, all against hated Green Bay. He scored a touchdown on an interception in the 73–0 shellacking of the Washington Redskins in the 1940 NFL Championship Game. He also played on the Bears' 1946 championship team after his time in the service.

McAfee was not an imposing figure, standing just under six feet tall and playing at about 177 pounds. But he was often called "unstoppable" with the football. He was also versatile, able to score as a runner, a passer, and a receiver. He was the league's best punter during his career, and punted left-footed, which was as rare then as it is today.

Playing behind Hall of Fame quarterback Sid Luckman, McAfee gained 5,313 yards in his career and scored 234 points. He was also the league's most dangerous punt returner and averaged 12.8 yards per punt in his career. He was also converted to a defensive backfield position and had 25 interceptions in his career.

He once said he ran so fast as a running back because he simply didn't want to get taken down. It looked like it might hurt.

He got into the Hall of Fame in large part because of what he did in 1941 before going to war. He scored 12 touchdowns in 11 games, with six on the ground, three as a receiver, one by punt return, one on a kickoff return, and one on an interception return. He averaged 7.3 yards per carry for the Bears as they won their second consecutive title just prior to the start of the war.

Red Grange, the most famous football player of his time, said McAfee was "the most dangerous man with the football in the game."

McAfee was credited with changing shoe styles in the NFL. He started wearing low-cut shoes rather than the high-top, tightly laced shoes that other players wore, saying that the low-cut shoe allowed him better movement on his cuts.

81 The Accident

Willie Galimore was fast. People who played with him said his speed was his best attribute as a football player. Most people who saw him said he was the fastest football player they had ever seen.

The Bears drafted Galimore out of Florida A&M University (he would later be elected to the College Football Hall of Fame) in the fifth round of the 1956 NFL Draft. He played with the Bears from 1956 to 1963, made the Pro Bowl one season, and was on the Bears' famed 1963 championship team.

In seven seasons with the Bears, he averaged 4.5 yards per carry, scored 26 touchdowns rushing, caught 87 passes, and had 10 touchdowns as a receiver. He also had one kickoff return for a touchdown. What made him special as a running back was his speed running laterally. It was said he could run as fast sideways as most runners could run going straight forward.

Galimore had improvisational skills with the football that made him unique. Some Bears observers said Galimore was Gale Sayers before Gale Sayers. His career was affected by injury, and he had double knee surgery before playing in the 1963 championship season.

He scored eight rushing touchdowns in the 1958 season, and he averaged a career-best 5.4 yards per carry in 1962. But that season was cut short because of his need for knee surgery. But in 1963 he averaged 3.8 yards per carry and scored five touchdowns, leading the Bears' offense as the team won the 1963 NFL championship. Bears fans were looking forward to the 1964 season knowing Galimore was coming back healthy and the Bears were going to do their best to defend the previous season's championship.

But the memory of Galimore as a Bear, and one of the reasons his number is retired, is not because of his prowess on the football field.

On the way back to their rooms at training camp in August of 1964, Galimore and teammate Bo Farrington were killed when their automobile flipped over just outside of St. Joseph's College in Rensselear, Indiana, where the Bears trained. Galimore was just 29 years old at the time.

Untimely death is sad for anyone, but Galimore was becoming invested in a serious cause. Prior to his death, Galimore participated in a civil rights activity in his hometown of St. Augustine, Florida. He used his fame from being with the Bears to help tear down some barriers in the racially divided South.

Many players from the 1963 team said the wind went out of the Bears' sails because of Galimore's passing. Although they had much the same lineup for the 1964 season, the Bears went just 5–9 that year, and as history tells us, they did not win another NFL title until Super Bowl XX.

82 Walter Payton as Receiver/Quarterback

Walter Payton was exuberant, active, boisterous, and always willing to put on a show.

But he was also quiet. He spoke in a very soft voice. He was sneaky. You always had to have your guard up when you were anywhere near where he might be. He liked to sneak behind people and surprise them. He loved snapping towels on the butts of unsuspecting reporters as well as teammates.

Eddie Payton

Imagine being the older brother of Walter Payton, and wanting to make your own name in the NFL. That's what life was like for Eddie Payton.

Eddie graduated from Jackson State in 1973 after playing running back for the Tigers. He was two inches shorter than Walter, standing 5'8" and weighing just 175 pounds. He was not drafted into the NFL after graduation.

Walter followed his brother onto the Jackson State team, and played alongside him for one season. Walter's career was much more successful at the college level, which is why he was drafted fourth overall by the Bears in 1975.

Once Walter established himself in the NFL, Eddie became more attractive, and signed a contract with the Cleveland Browns in 1977. He played two games for the Browns, then got cut and picked up by the Detroit Lions in the same season. While with the Lions, Eddie actually scored two touchdowns in the same game, one on a kickoff return and one on a punt return. He only had three touchdowns in his entire NFL career.

Eddie played for the Kansas City Chiefs in 1978 and for the Minnesota Vikings from 1980 to 1982. He played in 65 NFL games, and averaged 8.9 yards per punt return and 23.6 yards per kickoff return.

Eddie wore his brother's number 34 while with the Detroit Lions and Kansas City Chiefs.

Eddie wrote a book about his brother titled *Walter and Me: Standing in the Shadow of Sweetness*. The book was published in 2012 by Triumph Books.

So it comes as no surprise that, although he was best known for his ability to run the ball out of the backfield and find daylight, he was equally adept, and almost as dangerous, as a receiver. The idea was to get the ball into Payton's hands any way possible and let him do his magic.

In 13 seasons with the Bears, Payton caught 492 passes, almost 40 a season, and he scored 15 times as a receiver.

The key to his skill as a receiver was that he was small and, as said before, he was sneaky.

Payton was listed as 5'10", but that might have been generous. One reason he was so dangerous as a running back is that he was sometimes hard to see. He made himself small when he needed to.

For defensive players, the idea was to keep your eye on Payton at all times. But on those plays when the ball was not handed off to him and he suddenly became a receiver, the duties to keep the

Walter Payton catches a 33-yard touchdown behind two Redskin defenders in a September 1985 game. (Courtesy of Getty Images)

ball out of his hands fell to others. Payton could sneak into the defensive backfield, and his skill at finding open spaces made him a favorite target of quarterback Jim McMahon, who knew that once he delivered the ball, Payton would catch it.

For a small man, Payton had great hands. He could palm a football, often carrying it in one hand when the opportunity presented itself. People used to say it looked like he was holding a loaf of bread. As a drummer in his spare time, his hands were remarkably skilled.

In 1983, he caught 53 passes for 607 yards, both personal bests for him. That averaged to 11.5 yards per reception. He had the longest reception of his career, 75 yards, in 1977. In 1986, his next-to-last season in the NFL, he caught three touchdown passes to go with eight touchdowns scored on the ground.

Payton was also an adept passer. He threw eight touchdown passes in his career, an NFL record for non-quarterbacks in the modern era. He only completed 11 of 34 passes in his career, but he certainly made the completions count.

On October 21, 1979, Payton ran for a touchdown, caught a touchdown pass, and passed for a touchdown all in the same game against the Minnesota Vikings.

The thinking among the Bears was that Payton could play any position on the offensive side of the ball. He loved to block, and when called on to block for his fullback Matt Suhey or to keep defenders off of McMahon, his enthusiasm for that role seemed equal to his enthusiasm for running the ball.

"He is a complete football player," Bears general manager Jim Finks said.

Payton may have changed the definition of "complete football player."

83 George Connor

They didn't keep statistics to determine how many plays a player participated in back in the 1940s, but George Connor probably did not take many plays off.

Connor played offensive tackle, defensive tackle, and linebacker for the Bears from 1948 to 1955. He made All-Pro at each position at some point in his career.

As a college offensive tackle and linebacker, he was an All-American at Holy Cross and then a couple of years later at Notre Dame. He was a first-round draft pick of the New York Giants in 1946, but didn't play in the NFL until 1948 with the Chicago Bears, his hometown team.

Connor was a specimen. At 6'3" and 240 pounds, he was chiseled, but he was also unusually agile for a player his size. According to ChicagoBears.com, the most famous sportswriter of all time, Grantland Rice, said Connor was "the closest thing to a Greek god since Apollo."

It wasn't always that way. Born in Chicago in 1925, he weighed just three pounds at birth and there was a great amount of concern about whether he would survive his first year. He did, and it was late in high school that he finally grew to show his football potential.

He attended Holy Cross for two years at his parent's bequest, but after a stint in the Navy, he moved on to Notre Dame because of connections from his military service. In 1946, he was named the first winner of the Outland Trophy, given to the country's best lineman.

He had to play his way into the starting lineup while with the Bears, but he played in 11 of 12 games in his rookie year of 1948.

He started out playing on both lines, but in 1949, the Bears found themselves in need of a new kind of linebacker.

The Philadelphia Eagles were having success with a sweep play. The linebackers of the day were not able to do both things they needed to do—get to the outside and bring down the big running backs of the day. So the Bears moved the athletic Connor back to the linebacker position, and he turned out to be able to stymie the Eagles on the sweep play. He remained a linebacker from that point on.

Connor was a solid student while at both Holy Cross and Notre Dame and he displayed his intelligence on the football field. Connor was one of the first players to try to determine what the other team was going to do with the ball before the snap. He would study moves of offensive linemen and running backs to determine where the ball was going. He told other players not to watch the quarterback, because they could be deceiving. Linemen would let you know what was about to happen.

By 1950, the NFL had grown up and most players were specialists, playing on only one side of the ball, taking half the game off. Connor was one of the few players who remained active the entire game, and in 1951 and 1952, he was named to the All-NFL team as an offensive tackle and as a linebacker.

A knee injury kept him out of four games in 1954, but he came back to play all 12 games in 1955. He declared himself done in training camp in 1956.

Connor played 90 games for the Bears and had seven interceptions and 10 fumble recoveries. He was named to the Pro Football Hall of Fame in 1975. He lived in Chicago his entire life, and died in Chicago in 2003.

84 Bears vs. Packers

At the end of the 2019 season, the Chicago Bears and Green Bay Packers had played 200 games against each other. The Packers held a 99–95–6 record in the series. The competition between the two rivals is so significant to the NFL that when it celebrated its 100th season during the 2019 campaign, the first game of the season was a Bears-Packers game on Thursday, September 5.

They say that ties are like kissing your sister, but that's probably not the case in football games between the Bears and Packers.

The rivalry started in 1921 when the Packers bought into the NFL. The Bears and Packers have always played in the same conference or division, and have usually played each other twice in the regular season.

The Bears have the advantage in the series but the Packers have the most impressive win streaks.

From September of 1928 until November of 1930, the Packers did not lose in eight straight games. The streak started with a tie game and the Packers followed with seven consecutive wins.

The Bears actually won eight straight in the 1980s, starting with a pair of wins in the incredible 1985 season that ended with a Super Bowl championship.

Then came the mid-1990s, when the Packers were one of the most dominant teams in the league. They won 10 straight games in the series. They won three straight NFC Central championships in that time and one Super Bowl in 1996.

From the 1994 season through the 2004 season, the Packers won an amazing 19 out of 22 games in the series.

The 1960s did not go well for the Bears, either. The Packers had a 15–5 record in that decade, and two of the Bears' victories came in the championship season of 1963.

The only season in which the Bears and Packers did not play was the 1982 season when a player strike shortened the season.

There are almost as many opinions about the best games in the series as there are games in the series. But here are a few Bears fans will want to make sure they know all about:

December 14, 1941—the Packers beat the Bears during the 1941 regular season 16–14, and it was the only loss of the season for the Bears. The Bears and Packers both finished the season with 10–1–0 records, forcing a one-game playoff to determine the division champion. With the temperature at a brisk 16 degrees, the Bears hosted the Packers at Wrigley Field and recorded an easy 33–14 victory. The Bears won the 1941 title with a 37–9 victory over the New York Giants.

December 7, 1980—the Bears crushed the Packers 61–7, scoring eight touchdowns. Defensive coordinator Buddy Ryan, credited with the creation of the Bears defense that cruised to victory in Super Bowl XX, called on his defenders to blitz throughout the fourth quarter, causing Packers head coach Bart Starr to confront Bears head coach Neill Armstrong after the game.

November 5, 1989—there have been numerous times when the losing team in the series argued the other team cheated. This time, the Bears believed they had been cheated by the referees. In the final minute of the game, with the Bears winning 13–7, Green Bay Packers quarterback Don Majkowski completed a 14-yard touchdown pass to Sterling Sharpe, but it was immediately ruled that Majkowski had gone past the line of scrimmage before throwing the pass, nullifying the game-winning touchdown. The officials, however, decided on their own to review the play. They did not have to: it came before coaches had the opportunity to demand instant replay.

After reviewing the play, it was decided Majkowski had been behind the line of scrimmage when he threw the ball and the touchdown stood for a Packers' 14–13 win.

October 21, 1985—William Perry scored his first touchdown on a Monday night showcase game, with the Bears beating the Packers 23–7. Perry also blocked for Walter Payton on two touchdown runs in the game.

November 23, 1986—if there is ever an argument between Bears fans and Packers fans about which team plays the dirtiest, the Bears always point to this game to prove the Packers are the worst.

Bears quarterback Jim McMahon had just thrown an interception, which was bad enough. But as McMahon watched the end of the play, Packers defensive end Charles Martin came up from behind McMahon and picked him up, pinning his arm to his side. Martin then drove McMahon into the ground hard on his already sore shoulder. McMahon missed the rest of the season, and Martin immediately marked himself as the worst Packer ever in the eyes of the Chicago Bears.

While these are a few of the best games in the series, the truth is, for real Bears and Packers fans, every game between the two teams is the most important game of the season.

85 Chicago's Other Professional Football Teams

Since their inception, the Chicago Bears have been the top dog in Chicago professional football history. But there was another team in town, the Chicago Cardinals, who had their roots in the Chicago area even before the Bears got started, and stayed in town until 1960 when they left for St. Louis.

But even the Bears and Cardinals are not the only pro football teams in Chicago's history.

In 1926, Red Grange decided to make the most of his fame from the barnstorming tour he took with the Bears in 1925, and created the American Football League with his business partner C.C. Pyle as well as Joey Sternaman, the brother of Bears owner Dutch Sternaman. Grange played with the New York Yankees football team, but there was a team in Chicago and they were called the Bulls. They played their home games at Comiskey Park, forcing the Chicago Cardinals out of their home temporarily. The Bulls and the AFL lasted only one season.

The NFL has had serious challengers over the years, but none had the sustainability to compete for long. One of the first was the All-America Football Conference, which played its first season in 1946. Oddly, the league was founded by Arch Ward, the longtime sports editor of the *Chicago Tribune.*

The AAFC had eight teams initially, and one of them was the Chicago Rockets, owned by John L. Keeshin, a Chicago-area racetrack owner. Keeshin was anxious to get into sports ownership, even trying to buy the Chicago White Sox at one time. The AAFC was run by several men who had attempted to get into the NFL themselves but were rebuffed.

The new league actually stole players from the Bears and other NFL teams in a mad inflation of pro football player salaries. The San Francisco team grabbed fullback Norm Standlee, while tackle Lee Artoe and halfback Harry Clark went to Los Angeles.

AAFC teams also went after the Bears' stars, like Sid Luckman, Bulldog Turner, and George McAfee. Bears owner George Halas, notoriously cheap, refused to let his team be sandbagged by the newcomers and came up with the cash to increase salaries.

In 1948, a similar player-purge attempt caused Halas to pay Bobby Layne and Johnny Lujack large salaries to keep them from going to the AAFC.

Interestingly, the Chicago Rockets played their home games at Soldier Field, which the Bears avoided until 1971. In 1946, the Rockets were 5–6–3, but in 1947 and 1948 they went 1–13. They changed their name to the Chicago Hornets in 1949 but that didn't help much as they went 4–8.

The Rockets played against the Brooklyn Dodgers, Buffalo Bisons, Cleveland Browns, Los Angeles Dons, Miami Seahawks, New York Yankees, and San Francisco 49ers. In 1950, the NFL absorbed three AAFC franchises, the ones in Cleveland, San Francisco, and Baltimore. Since the league already had two teams in the Bears and Cardinals, it had no interest in accepting a third team.

In 1961, the United Football League offered minor league professional football, and had a team in Chicago for just one season. The Chicago Bulls, again, went 1–11 in 1962 and disbanded. Growing out of the United Football League was the Continental Football League.

The Continental Football League started in 1965 and was comprised mostly of former minor league clubs, although the intent of the league was to become a major player and compete against the NFL and newly formed American Football League. But the CFL did not have a Chicago franchise until 1968, when the Chicago Owls were formed.

The Owls played just two seasons in the CFL, which disbanded after the 1969 season, when it had 22 teams and four divisions, reaching as far as Honolulu and Mexico. But the Owls had the distinction of preceding the Bears into Soldier Field, just as the Chicago Rockets did.

In 1974, a new operation called the World Football League started with plans to create teams outside of the United States as well as American franchises. The Chicago Fire played in the WFL, and the team played in Soldier Field. The Fire lost its last 11 games and folded immediately after the season.

The WFL awarded another franchise to Chicago, and the team was known as the Chicago Winds, and also played at Soldier Field. The Winds had poor attendance and financial problems and folded in midseason.

In 1983, a very aggressive attempt was made to compete with the NFL, which had absorbed the AFL in the 1960s and was growing into the most dominant sports league in America. The United States Football League (USFL) was supposed to play its games in the spring and the summer to provide an alternative to the NFL.

The Chicago market had a team in the USFL named the Chicago Blitz and owned by a well-known heart surgeon named Ted Diethrich. George Allen, the former assistant coach of the Bears and a former head coach in the NFL, became the head coach of the Blitz.

Because they played in the spring, Soldier Field was more than happy to host them, since the stadium had few if any spring clients by the 1980s.

Allen put together a significant roster of talent for the first season, and the 1983 Blitz went 12–6 and ended up tied with the

Michigan Panthers for the Central Division regular season title. A tiebreaker went against them and they ended up in the first season wild-card playoff game, which they lost to the Philadelphia Stars in overtime.

For the 1984 season, Diethrich wanted out of Chicago, and sold his team to a Milwaukee heart surgeon named James Hoffman. Diethrich then bought the Arizona Wranglers of the USFL. Almost immediately after that, Hoffman and Diethrich agreed to trade all assets of the two teams, so the Wranglers got all the Blitz players and the Blitz got all the Wrangler players. Not a great deal for Chicago, since the Wranglers were 4–14 in their first season.

The 1984 Blitz went 5–13 and folded before the 1985 season, when the league decided to challenge the NFL by playing in the fall.

In 2001, yet another league came along to challenge the NFL, which by that time had reached epic proportions of power in the United States. The new league was called the XFL, and was the brainchild of a man named Vince McMahon, who was the owner of World Wrestling Entertainment. The Chicago Enforcers were one of the eight teams in the XFL, and they went 5–5 in their first and only season of play, with home games at Soldier Field.

The XFL owned all of its eight teams, so there was no Chicago owner to the team. Former Bears linebacker Dick Butkus was initially hired to coach the team but moved to the league's front office before the first game. Former college coach Ron Meyer coached the team.

86 Halas Saves Green Bay

George Halas, owner of the Bears, had a healthy respect for the Green Bay Packers. He knew the Bears would be better served to have a healthy rival like the Packers, and kept the lines of communication open between the two teams for the purposes of making the NFL stronger and more solvent on and off the field.

But, throughout their existence, the Packers had financial problems. In their first three seasons, founder and coach Curly Lambeau had to find three sets of financial backers to allow them to get into the NFL in the first place. The first was the Indian Packing Company, for whom Lambeau worked, and that is how they got their name.

In 1922, a group called the Hungry Five, a group of local businessmen, backed the team financially. They created the Green Bay Football Corporation, a publicly owned group that allowed residents to invest in the team. The local ownership idea created a unique system that helped keep the Packers in Green Bay and made them the all-time best small-market team in any professional league.

But in 1956, the NFL was pressuring the Green Bay Football Corporation to build a new stadium. Television and big business was pushing the league into new areas of growth. Green Bay was not keeping up. The league was talking about relocating the Packers somewhere else.

The Packers' original home, City Stadium, located on the city's east side, seated only 25,000 fans. That wasn't nearly enough to satisfy the needs of the NFL.

The city needed funds to build a new stadium, and residents were balking at the price tag, which required a new bond to be issued to create a fund of $1 million toward the new stadium.

A rally was held in Green Bay early in 1956, and a surprise visitor to the rally was Bears owner and coach George Halas, who made an impassioned plea to city citizens and local business officials to pass the stadium referendum. When the vote passed, Halas and his words of encouragement were given much of the credit.

When the Packers applied to join the NFL in 1921, it was Halas who stated the case that the Packers would be a good addition to the league. When the Packers were kicked out of the league for signing college players prior to the end of their college eligibility it was Halas who urged the league to allow the Packers to return.

Of course, it was Halas who turned the Packers in for breaking the league rules on college players, but that was more gamesmanship than anything else.

Years later, Halas also had a role in the NFL's initial program for revenue sharing, which was a way to keep the league's smaller markets viable and competitive against the larger markets. Green Bay was the main and most notable recipient of the plan.

87 The Bears Go to London

If you were not alive or not aware of what was going on with the Super Bowl XX champion Chicago Bears, you have no idea how large the team was in terms of personality and popularity. They were bigger than any sports team before them. There have been few teams bigger than them since.

The Bears were huge before they beat the New England Patriots in Super Bowl XX. They had already filmed "The Super Bowl Shuffle." The nation already knew how great the defense was. Everybody watched them lose their one regular season game in Miami. Everybody knew they were going to win the Super Bowl. When they won the game by 36 points, no one was surprised.

So, when the Bears arrived in London in the late summer of 1986 for the first American Bowl, it should come as no surprise that it was compared to the Beatles' invasion of the United States. Led by the remarkably popular William "the Refrigerator" Perry, the Bears took over London like few American sports teams have ever done in a foreign land.

The Bears were in London to prepare for an exhibition game against the Dallas Cowboys. The Cowboys were still coached by Tom Landry at the time, and were known as America's team. But the Bears were proving to be the World's Team.

The NFL had been in London previously. The Minnesota Vikings and St. Louis Cardinals played in Wembley Stadium in 1983, but there was very little fanfare. Both teams arrived only one day before the game, and the stadium did not sell out for that game.

In 1986, as the NFL started its American Bowl series (which sent NFL teams around the world until 2005 for preseason games) there was a lot of hoopla surrounding the Bears' appearance. The Bears showed up one week before the game and reporters were trying to get a word with Perry, Walter Payton, Jim McMahon, Richard Dent, Steve McMichael, or coach Mike Ditka.

The Bears were popular in England because the country had discovered the NFL. The Super Bowl had grown in popularity across the pond to the point that it got the same kind of viewing audience as the best soccer games in the English Premier League.

A sellout crowd watched the Bears beat the Cowboys 17–6, and a new audience was enthralled.

The Bears played in two more American Bowl games, losing to the San Francisco 49ers 21–7 in Berlin in 1991, and losing again to the Pittsburgh Steelers in Dublin in 1997.

Eventually, the NFL decided to start playing regular season games in new, international venues. The Bears played a regular season game in Toronto during the 2010 season, beating the Buffalo Bills 22–19. Because the Bears are such an international brand, they were once again asked to play far from home and were the visiting team against the Tampa Bay Buccaneers in a game in London's Wembley Stadium again on October 23, 2011.

Brian Urlacher, Jay Cutler, and the other Bears again invaded London, participating in a cricket practice at one point, and being seen moving around the top tourist attractions in the city. Players showed up at a fan rally in Trafalgar Square, and a group of players visited Buckingham Palace.

The Bears only showed up Friday for the Sunday game, which was played before 76,981 fans at Wembley, but they were far more popular than the Buccaneers, who showed up a week early for the contest.

The Bears won the game 24–18. They did so with their signature component—defense—intercepting four passes, and allowing just 30 yards on the ground.

There is no way to know just what the English audience thought of the Bears' powerful defense, but the NFL continues to grow in markets outside the United States and the Bears are a key reason why.

88 Why Didn't Payton Score?

There are many things Bears fans need to know about Super Bowl XX. You need to know the Bears were 15–1 in the regular season, the one loss coming at Miami. You need to know the Bears pitched shutouts in the two playoff games before the Super Bowl. You need to know the Bears won the Super Bowl 46–10 in what was the biggest blowout in Super Bowl history at that time.

And you need to know one more thing—Walter Payton, the heart and soul of the team and one of the best offensive players in Bears history, did not score in the game, despite the fact the Bears had five touchdowns.

Fullback Matt Suhey scored on an 11-yard run in the first quarter. Quarterback Jim McMahon had a two-yard touchdown run and a one-yard touchdown run. Reggie Phillips scored on a 28-yard interception return. William Perry, the defensive lineman, was called on to chug into the end zone on a one-yard run in the third quarter.

Payton ended up with 61 yards on 22 carries and no scores.

For his part, Bears coach Mike Ditka said after the game and for years later that he regretted not finding a way to get Payton a touchdown.

"I guess if I have one regret, I would've made sure Walter Payton scored a touchdown in the Super Bowl," Ditka said in an ESPN interview. "That was the only thing that ever came back to haunt me, the fact that he never scored. I never thought about it. I really didn't. He was such a great guy and a great player, and I never realized how much it meant to him."

"Actually, he was kind of a decoy in that game," he said. "Everything that New England did was keyed to him, so we kind

The Fridge spikes the ball after rumbling for a one-yard touchdown in Super Bowl XX. (Courtesy of Getty Images)

of used Suhey as the guy to run the ball. So that's the only regret I have."

"I knew I was going to be a decoy today and I was prepared for it," Payton said in his postgame interviews. But he was visibly upset as the game drew to a close and he was not responsible for any of the points.

Payton, in fact, did not score through the entire playoffs that season. The Bears beat the New York Giants in the divisional playoff 21–0 and beat the Los Angeles Rams 24–0 in the NFC title game but Payton did not score in either of those contests either.

In the Super Bowl, Payton did have his chances to score.

In the first quarter, the Bears got down to the 3-yard line but Ditka called for a halfback option to be run by Perry, who was tackled on the play for a loss. The Bears settled for a field goal.

Payton probably could have scored on either of McMahon's touchdowns, although he was used as the decoy on both as part of an option play. Just before McMahon's first touchdown, Payton had a two-yard carry from the 4-yard line. He was tackled for a two-yard loss on a running play from inside the 5-yard line in the first quarter. Payton was behind Perry when he scored the third-quarter touchdown and with Perry blocking for him he probably could have gotten into the end zone.

After the game, Payton celebrated the victory but expressed disappointment he was not able to score a touchdown. It took very little time for him to release that disappointment and he rarely spoke of it again.

89 Jay Berwanger

Although George Halas was very careful with his money, he rarely lost out on talent that he wanted for his football team. There is no telling what might have happened if he had won one of the most famous negotiating battles he ever lost.

In 1935, a running back from the University of Chicago named Jay Berwanger won the first Downtown Athletic Club Trophy as the outstanding college football player in the land. The next year that award was renamed the Heisman Trophy, putting Berwanger first on the list of Heisman Trophy winners. He received a trip for two to New York for the presentation.

Berwanger did everything for the Maroons. He played quarterback, although he was listed as a halfback. He kicked punts and extra points, he was also a strong defensive lineman on the opposite side of the ball.

While in college, Berwanger not only competed in football but he was also a champion in track and field, competing in the most grueling of events, the decathlon.

The NFL was relatively healthy in 1936, but it certainly wanted to have the nation's best college player in its ranks. The NFL was instituting its first draft of college players that year, and Berwanger went first, selected by the Philadelphia Eagles.

Berwanger made it clear to the Eagles that he wanted $1,000 per game. The Eagles did not want to pay that for one player and traded the rights to Berwanger to the Chicago Bears.

Negotiations between the Bears and Berwanger were put off through the summer of 1936 because Berwanger wanted to try to make the United States Olympic track team to compete in the decathlon, and signing a pro football contract would have made him ineligible.

Berwanger did not make the Olympic team, and began negotiating with Halas, who was very familiar with Berwanger. Halas often attended University of Chicago games, and was aware that adding Berwanger would be a public relations coup for the Bears.

Berwanger wanted $25,000 for a two-year contract, and Halas would not match that total. Berwanger did not sign. He went to work for a Chicago manufacturing company and worked part-time as a coach at the University of Chicago. He never played professional football.

For a short while, Berwanger wrote a sports column for the *Daily News* in Chicago. He actually played himself in a movie titled *The Big Game.* He coached the Maroons for four seasons.

Berwanger was enshrined in the College Football Hall of Fame in 1954.

As for the Downtown Athletic Club trophy itself, Berwanger was not afraid to admit he used it as a door stop in his home, because it was quite hefty. Eventually he donated it to the University of Chicago.

Later in life, Berwanger admitted he regretted not coming to an agreement with Halas to play for the Bears.

The Bears have only ever drafted two Heisman Trophy winners. The first time was when they selected Johnny Lujack out of Notre Dame in the 1946 collegiate draft, and the second was the selection of Rashaan Salaam out of the University of Colorado in 1995.

90 Al Harris and Todd Bell

There is nothing worse than "missing out." When an opportunity presents itself for a life-changing event, and you don't make the most of that opportunity, it's the kind of thing that can dog you forever.

Such was the case for two members of the Chicago Bears, who were on the team in 1984, and could have been on the team in 1985 all the way through the greatest Super Bowl championship of all time. But they chose not to be involved due to a dispute with the team over money, and they missed out on the chance to be part of history.

Al Harris and Todd Bell were key contributors to the 1984 Chicago Bears team that went 10–6. They were supposed to be on the 1985 team but were not. These are their stories.

Al Harris was an All-American defensive end and linebacker at Arizona State. The Bears selected him in the first round of the 1979 NFL Draft. From 1979 to 1984 he started 45 games, including all 16 in the 1984 season. He had 11.5 sacks (since 1982, when sacks were first recorded) and a pair of interceptions, including one for a touchdown.

Harris was comparing himself to Bears linebacker Wilber Marshall, and wanted to be paid $1 more than Marshall because Harris felt he had outplayed Marshall during the 1984 season. The Bears offered Harris $825,000 for three years, but Marshall was making $925,000 a year thanks to the fact that the Bears had to negotiate against the USFL, which had also drafted him. Harris felt betrayed and disrespected. He held out for the entire season.

Todd Bell was a safety out of Ohio State. The Bears selected him in the fourth round of the 1981 NFL Draft, and by 1984 he was a Pro Bowl selection. He became a favorite player of defensive coordinator Buddy Ryan because of his hard hits. He had 4.5 sacks and four interceptions in 1984, including one for a touchdown.

Bell was looking for an increase from his annual salary of $77,000 to $950,000, which was more than any other player on the team was making at the time. The Bears offered $1.6 million for four years, but the money was not guaranteed, meaning he would be playing for his contract and money every year.

The Bears were a family-run operation, based on the directives of Papa Bear George Halas, who had died two years earlier. There was a family feel to the group, even though the business side of the game did get in the way.

Jerry Vainisi, a longtime employee of the team who had been moved to the general manager's role, said he felt he let down both the team and the players by failing to come to an agreement. He told ESPN it was "one of my dark memories as general manager."

At one point, Vainisi turned to the parents of both Harris and Bell, trying to get them back in the fold so they could participate in the 1985 season, which everyone believed was going to be special.

Both players had until November 23 to sign, but neither did. At that point the Bears were 11–0 and looking like the giants they turned out to be. Bell requested a trade but the Bears did not comply. The Bears actually arranged a trade for Harris but he had to sign the contract first and would not do so.

Dave Duerson replaced Bell in the starting lineup at safety, and Marshall was easily moved into Harris' starting linebacker role. Duerson said he had to play the entire season trying to prove himself to Ryan, who was not shy about saying he preferred Bell in that role.

Because Harris and Bell held out and missed out on what would have been the greatest season in their professional careers, few people remember that defensive end Richard Dent and linebacker Mike Singletary were both in difficult negotiations with the club for contract extensions. They both decided to play through the conflict, and Dent said it was the fuel that he used to have a great season that ended with him being the Super Bowl MVP.

Bell and Harris both came to agreements with the team for the 1986 season, when most felt the Bears were a likely candidate to repeat their Super Bowl success. But the team suffered injury problems, and did not advance to the championship game in 1986—or again until 2006.

When Ryan left the Bears after the 1985 season to become head coach of the Philadelphia Eagles, he eventually signed both Bell and Harris to his team, Bell in 1988 and Harris in 1989.

91 George Allen

The story of George Allen's time with the Chicago Bears is one of allegiance and perceived betrayal.

George Allen was coaching at Whittier College, a small college in California, when he was asked to join the Los Angeles Rams staff in 1957. In 1958, when Allen was out of football, he was hired by George Halas to serve on the Bears' staff, and his main responsibility was to scout the Rams. Allen had an eye for defense, and his scouting reports on the Rams' offensive tendencies were so impressive, Halas eventually offered him a full-time job on the defensive staff.

Allen eventually worked his way up to the head of the defense for the Bears, and in doing so replaced longtime Bears coach and Halas friend Clark Shaughnessy, who had brought the T-formation to the Bears in the 1940s. Allen became famous for his defensive strategies, and with the help of athletic giants such as Bill George at linebacker and Doug Atkins at defensive end, he produced the defense that led the Bears to the 1963 NFL championship. Under Allen's leadership, the Bears gave up just 144 points in 14 games.

Allen also had responsibility for the team's draft choices while he was with the team, and while he was in charge, the Bears drafted three future Hall of Famers in Mike Ditka, Gale Sayers, and Dick Butkus. Sayers and Butkus came to the Bears in the same round of the same draft in 1965.

Halas was getting up there in years, and arthritis was taking a toll on his body. He was going to eventually have to step down as coach, and it was his plan to have Allen replace him. But Allen could not wait, and after the 1965 season, he was willing to listen to other teams in search of a head coach.

Allen eventually signed a contract with the Los Angeles Rams to coach their team for the 1966 season. But Halas immediately filed a lawsuit saying Allen had a contract with the Bears. The suit was filed in Chicago, and Halas got a favorable verdict, but as soon as the verdict was handed down, Halas released Allen from his Bears contract, saying he only wanted to prove that the contract he had was valid.

But Halas was clearly upset with Allen's decision, and never spoke a kind word about Allen after that.

The Rams went 8–6 in Allen's first year with the team, then went 11–1–2 in 1967, earning Allen Coach of the Year honors. Still, Allen was a contentious coach, and had arguments with Rams owner Dan Reeves, at one point getting fired despite having a winning record following the 1968 season. But the entire team of players held a press conference after the firing, making a public plea to Reeves to reconsider and rehire Allen. Reeves did in fact give Allen a new contract, however in the two years that followed, the Rams made the playoffs once but were unable to win a title, and Allen left the Rams after the 1970 season.

Allen then went on to coach the Washington Redskins for seven seasons, making the playoffs five times and getting to Super Bowl VII, where his team lost to the Miami Dolphins. His Redskins never had a losing record, but when he failed to make the playoffs in 1977, he could not come to agreement with Redskins management on a new deal. He went back to coach the Rams, but his coaching and leadership style was no longer appreciated by modern players, and after a player revolt, he was dismissed at the end of the 1978 exhibition season by the Rams.

In 1983, he returned to Chicago to coach the Chicago Blitz of the United States Football League. He led them to a 12–6 record but they lost in a playoff game.

In 12 NFL seasons, Allen had a record of 116–47–5. He never had a losing record as an NFL coach.

Halas retired as coach of the Bears after the 1967 season, two years after Allen left the Bears for the Rams. Allen could have coached the Bears if he had waited two years, or Halas had moved on two years earlier. Instead, Allen went elsewhere, and the Bears' fortunes suffered for 22 years without a championship.

92 The Quarterback Club

There are many things to brag about when you are a Chicago Bears fan: the historical defenses; the heritage stemming from the life of George Halas; the memory of great players like Walter Payton, Dick Butkus, and Gale Sayers; the history of the team from the beginning in 1920.

But quarterback has never been a long-term strength. When they acquired Jay Cutler in 2009 he was declared one of the top quarterbacks in Bears' history although he had never won anything.

But in 1948, the Bears had three quarterbacks—yes, three—that were future Hall of Famers. They didn't get to use all three as quarterback, and two of them made their names primarily with other teams. But for one brief shining moment, Chicago was host to the Quarterback Club.

In 1946, the Bears drafted Johnny Lujack from the University of Notre Dame. They actually selected him before he was eligible to join the NFL and he didn't play for the team until 1948.

In 1948, the Bears had the good fortune to draft Bobby Layne, a quarterback out of Texas, with the third pick in the draft. They had acquired the pick through a couple of player exchanges with the Detroit Lions. Keep the Lions in mind for future reference.

Lujack and Layne joined Sid Luckman, widely considered the most effective quarterback in Bears history. Luckman was only 31 at the time, but Bears owner George Halas was preparing for future needs.

At the time of Layne joining the team, the new All-America Football Conference was trying to make headway in the United States by signing players to exorbitant contracts. Halas gave Layne a three-year deal worth $22,500 a year, and paid Lujack $18,000 for his first year, just to keep them from jumping to the AAFC.

In 1948, Luckman started, Lujack played second string, and Layne played third. Luckman started eight games, Lujack started three, and Layne got into 11 of the 12 games played that season. Luckman threw 13 touchdown passes, Lujack had six, and Layne had three. The Bears went 10–2 that season but did not make the championship game.

Halas could not handle the thought of all the money he had sitting on the bench when Luckman was playing, so he had to get rid of one of his extra quarterbacks. He traded Layne to the New York Bulldogs for $50,000 and two draft choices. It was considered one of the biggest trades in NFL history at the time.

Layne played one year for New York then got traded to Detroit, where he played eight-plus seasons, throwing 118 touchdown passes and winning three NFL titles. In all he played 15 years in the NFL and was inducted into the Pro Football Hall of Fame in 1967.

But Halas had a replacement for Layne. In 1949, Halas selected George Blanda out of Kentucky in the 12th round of the NFL Draft. Blanda was a quarterback and placekicker. He eventually started 26 games at quarterback for the Bears over 10 seasons, although his claim to fame with the team was as a kicker. He eventually scored 541 points with the Bears, with 88 field goals and 247 extra points to go with five rushing touchdowns. He also threw 48 touchdown passes for the Bears.

In 1949, Lujack replaced Luckman as the starting quarterback and had seven starts with 23 touchdowns. This time it was Luckman and Blanda who sat out. Blanda contributed seven field goals that season.

By 1950, Lujack was in his prime and Luckman was ready to retire. Blanda was nothing more than a placekicker.

Blanda finally got his chance to run the Bears offense in 1953, but he had 14 touchdowns to 23 interceptions that year. He got injured the next season and his career in the NFL was over, at least for a while. He eventually came back to play for the Houston Oilers and Oakland Raiders of the American Football League, then rejoined the NFL when the AFL and NFL merged. He won two AFL titles with the Oilers, and played in Super Bowl II with the Raiders.

Blanda eventually set records for seasons (26) and games played (340).

So, from 1948 to 1953, the Bears had four quarterbacks who combined for 610 NFL touchdown passes. Unfortunately, most of them were for other teams.

93 Walking Around Soldier Field

When Soldier Field underwent its renovation at the start of the 21st century, it was imperative that the location retain its memorial status for the World War I and II soldiers who were honored by its existence.

Although it now has the modern center that looms high over its historic exterior, there is still a lot to look at on the outside of the stadium. Once you get inside, though, there actually still are details that remain from the original stadium design.

From the outside, from a distance, you can still see the colonnades that are on both the east and west sides of the stadium. The colonnades are series of columns, several feet apart, that create a patio that is used for team events and can also be used for private parties or gatherings. At Soldier Field, there are 32 columns on each side of the stadium that create the colonnades. From both the inside and outside, they bring to mind the famous stadiums of the great ancient cultures of Rome and Greece.

Fans can walk around Soldier Field and see the way the stadium has looked since it was built. Although the south end includes a huge outdoor parking lot, farther south is the famed McCormick Place Convention Center.

Walking around to the east side, there is Lake Michigan, which is a beautiful view from anywhere on the Chicago lakefront. Northeast of Soldier Field is the Adler Planetarium, one of the oldest and most famous stargazing facilities in the United States. West of the Adler Planetarium is Chicago's famed Shedd Aquarium.

Walking on the north side of Soldier Field, you are between the stadium and the Field Museum of Natural History. The entertainment opportunities on a visit to Soldier Field could provide an entire day's activities.

There is also a 15-foot stand-alone sculpture installed in 2003 titled "A Tribute to Freedom." It's a presentation of soldiers and sailors from World War I, surrounded by their families. There are 12 figures in all, and it serves as a constant reminder of the service of others and the people who wait for them at home. The sculpture has the words "Dedicated to the Defenders and Their Families" inscribed on the face.

On the west side of the stadium is Lake Shore Drive, one of Chicago's best-known roadways. To the west of that is Michigan Avenue, another well-known thoroughfare.

If you have tickets to a Bears game, you need to get there early to enjoy more of the history inside. Presented by the Bears to the city are two sculptures inside the stadium. Just inside Gate 15 is a 26-foot-high sculpture which is attached to the wall and depicts

George Halas as both player and coach. He is bordered by some of the most famous players to play for the Bears, including Red Grange, Bronko Nagurski, Walter Payton, and Dick Butkus.

On the other side of the stadium, inside Gate 0, is a statue of a Doughboy, which is what the grunt soldiers from World War I were called.

Once you get past the initial set of walls inside, the stadium is brand new. The entire interior was redone in the renovation in 2002. But the exterior is a reminder of the way things were in Chicago, and may always be.

94 Walter Payton the Prankster

Walter Payton was always smiling. Sometimes, when he was enjoying himself, it was a broad smile, and sometimes, when he was about to *really* enjoy himself, it was a sly smile.

For all of his admirable character traits, like drive, desire, work ethic, and gamesmanship, the one trait that was as strong as the others but rarely exhibited in public was his playful sense of humor.

It might be hard to believe of one of the greatest running backs in the history of the NFL, not to mention one of the greatest competitors in league history, but Walter Payton absolutely loved pulling pranks on teammates and team officials. One of his favorite pranks, the one that made entering the Bears locker room dangerous, was to wrap a wet towel around itself, turning it into a weapon, and then snapping the towel on the butt of anyone who dared allow Payton to stand behind him.

The towel snap was most effective on teammates coming out of showers, of course, but Payton not only snapped teammates, he snapped coaches and really enjoyed getting members of the media who worked the locker rooms.

Nothing was sacred or safe around Payton. He spiked water bottles. He liked to wake up teammates at training camp by setting off fireworks in the middle of the night. Whenever he heard a ringing phone, he answered it, and had full conversations with people who had no idea to whom they were speaking. He especially enjoyed answering the phone at the receptionist desk at Halas Hall. His soft, almost feminine voice made that prank easier to pull off.

When the Bears would practice in the cold and snow of Chicago's early winters, Payton would race to the locker room at the end of the workout so he could lock the doors and keep his teammates and coaches outside.

Payton rarely took interviews seriously. He would smile at almost all questions, and his responses weren't usually very usable from a reporter's standpoint, but they were usually unusual. It was hard to get him to stand still long enough to have a meaningful interview.

When Doug Flutie joined the Bears in 1986, he was surprised to find out that Payton was just as playful in games as he was out of games.

"During the playoffs, he would pull my socks down in the huddle," Flutie said.

Walter Payton had a *joie de vivre* that was authentic. He was someone you wanted to be around. Having him show up in a room changed the atmosphere of the room and the demeanor of everyone in it.

"As a person, he was a bright spot for any darkness that appeared," former teammate Mike Singletary said.

In the end, Walter Payton was a player you couldn't look away from on the field—and a man you didn't want to look away from off the field.

95 Mascots/Cheerleaders

It's not unusual for the Chicago Bears to have a mascot, which is a human being inside a very friendly, rotund Bear uniform. What's unusual is that they went so long without one.

From the beginning of the Bears, the franchise always had diehard fans. When television coverage rolled around, some fans took their appreciation of the team to a new level, wearing outlandish versions of the Bears uniform, and making a spectacle of themselves as cheerleaders and rabble-rousers.

Face paint became a big thing in the 1980s, and of course, because it's Chicago and sometimes the games are played in very cold weather, some fans make their allegiance known by printing the letters to the word "Bears" across their chests, which they display without concern for the temperature. It's imperative that you have five people in your group so the word can be properly displayed.

But the Bears did not have an official mascot until 2003, when they finally adopted a bear who wears a Bears jersey, No. 00, with his name on the back. His name is Staley Da Bear, which hails back to the beginnings of the franchise when it was known as the Decatur Staleys (the company that first owned the team was named Staley). The "Da Bear" portion relates to a famed *Saturday Night Live* skit making fun of the way Chicago Bears fans talk.

Staley Da Bear gets the crowd going before a 2009 game against the Packers.
(Courtesy of Getty Images)

Staley is ever-present at Bears games, and is a lot of fun for the younger fans. He is not a stunt mascot, however, as he is a little too round to do a lot of jumping. He does dance, however.

Once the Bears got around to creating a mascot, they wasted no time in making him popular with the children in the form of souvenirs. Staley bears can be found in teddy bear style, as footwear, as hats, and as Christmas ornaments.

The Bears offer Staley as a teacher. He goes to area schools and teaches the next generation of mascot performers how to do their jobs.

The Bears did have an unofficial mascot for a number of years prior to the "birth" of Staley.

A Bears fan and season-ticket holder named Don Wachter would show up at games in quite the getup. He wore face paint, had a No. 46 jersey on in honor of former Bears safety Doug Plank, and had a Bears coonskin-style hat on his head. He also wore shoulder pads under his jersey, and had "bear" paws on his hands and feet. He entertained fans in his seating area for years.

According to BearsHistory.com,Wachter eventually asked the Bears in 1995 if he could participate in some official capacity in game situations. The Bears allowed him on the field, and he would run across the field carrying a massive Bears flag every time the team scored. He also ran out in front of the team as they took to the field before each half.

Wachter managed to turn this obsession and behavior into a memorable part of the Bears experience. He appeared in numerous television commercials and was almost always seen during Bears telecasts. When Staley showed up, Wachter was sent back to his seats.

For 10 seasons, the Bears also had an official cheerleading squad. From 1976 to 1985, the Honey Bears strolled the sidelines for Bears home games. Coached by Cathy Core, who moved on from the Bears to help create the popular LuvaBulls for the Chicago Bulls, the Honey Bears were beautiful and, when weather allowed, wore relatively risqué cheerleader uniforms while revving up the crowd at Soldier Field.

The Honey Bears were originally the idea of owner George Halas. Ironically, it was his daughter, Virginia McCaskey, who nixed the Honey Bears after the team won Super Bowl XX, believing the cheerleaders did not fit the team image, although there were some who thought the decision was based on a sense of morality.

Since the Honey Bears' last appearance was at Super Bowl XX, and the Bears have not won a Super Bowl since, some believe there may be a Honey Bear curse on the team.

96 Walter Payton's Hill

When Walter Payton moved from Mississippi to Chicago to join the Bears in 1975, the most famous thing he brought with him was his training regimen.

Payton was a physical marvel. Although he stood just 5'10", he officially was listed as a 200-pounder, and it was all muscle. His thighs were massive. His strength was unbelievable, especially in light of his maneuverability. His physical presence was felt in every play on the field, as he churned up ground as a running back and punished defenders who tried to stop him. Likewise, as a blocker, he was far more powerful than any man his size had any right to be.

When Payton was at Jackson State University, he started a personal training regimen that included a very painful procedure;

he would find a very steep hill and run up it as hard as he possibly could, time and again. It produced the desired results, which was the strength in his legs, but it was hard to imagine the personal will required to go through the process the way he did.

When he arrived in Chicago, he moved to Arlington Heights, a northwest suburb of the city, and found a steep hill near a landfill that was not being used for any purpose. Just as he did back home, Payton took to the hill on a regular basis as part of his preparation for NFL seasons. He would run as hard as he could up that hill, building the powerful leg muscles that almost defined description. They were tree trunks, holding up his muscular 5'10" frame.

Thanks to the gift of the Internet, you can watch Payton do his hill workout. There are a couple of videos that not only show him running the hill, but also have him describing the effect of the workout, and the challenge it presented him.

One video clip is from a television interview done on Payton's personal training regimen. Payton is shown running up the hill and discussing the workout.

"Once you get halfway, you think 'I could stop,' but the angle is so steep that once you stop, it's harder to get started again. And when you go down, you are not in control. The hill controls you," Payton said.

Payton said he invited teammates to work out with him at the hill but that they eventually all just threw up trying to keep up with him.

The workout worked. Payton was a remarkable physical specimen.

"He is as solid physically as anyone I have ever seen," Ditka said.

Walter Payton's "hill" no longer exists. It was replaced by the Nickol Knoll Golf Club, a par-3 course that still celebrates Payton's dedication to fitness by marking the site of his favorite workout incline. There are two plaques commemorating Payton's efforts there. The clubhouse also includes photos and memorabilia from the Payton era.

97 Uniforms

The Chicago Bears' uniforms are blue and orange because George Halas went to the University of Illinois collegiately and really liked the colors the Ilini used.

So we have Halas to blame when the Bears decide to play in orange jerseys.

In 2013, the Bears wear blue jerseys with white pants, white shirt with blue pants, as well as all-white and all-blue uniforms. They use their orange jersey in one game a year, usually around Halloween.

Although most uniform kits for the Bears today involve the colors blue and white, they did experiment with an orange jersey as early as 1933, although it was not the usual uniform choice of the team.

The orange jersey was shelved by the 1940s, but showed up again in 2005 as the NFL began expanding into alternative kits in much the way the NBA and Major League Baseball were doing at the same time. The orange jersey is used with the white pants.

Stripes play a big role in the Chicago Bears uniform. On the sleeve of the jersey, there are three stripes on each side. There is also a stripe running down both sides of the pants.

Since 1991, the NFL has requested and/or allowed teams to use throwback jerseys on occasion. This allows teams to honor their squads from years past, and shows new fans and young fans what football uniforms looked like back in the day. It's also a way to market new jerseys to an audience that has already bought up the entire current uniform product available.

The first Bears' throwback jerseys were replicas of the original uniforms from 1920, which were blue and brown, as orange was not an easy color to produce in mass quantity. The originals were also wool jerseys and leather pants, which the throwbacks did not copy.

The Bears have also worn throwback jerseys from the 1940s when the Monsters of the Midway were winning championships consistently.

In the 1940s, the Bears actually wore black jerseys with orange numbers.

Players names were added to the jerseys in 1970 and in 1983, after the death of George Halas, a football-shaped patch bearing the initials GSH was sewn into each jersey. That patch remains on the uniform today.

98 Edward "Dutch" Sternaman

There is no more famous name in all of football than "Halas." It is the name that for most people signals the beginning of football in this country, at least at the professional level. The Chicago Bears and the name "Halas" are nearly synonymous.

The name "Sternaman" has virtually no cache in football except with historians. Yet, there was a "Sternaman" who was with Halas for the first 12 years of the Bears existence and had just as much meaning to the beginning of the franchise and the NFL as Halas did.

Edward Sternaman, known to friends as "Dutch," was a teammate of George Halas on the University of Illinois football team. When they graduated from college in 1919, they both went to work for the A.E. Staley Company located in Decatur, Illinois. The Staley Company manufactured starch from corn.

Back at the start of the 20th century, companies would sponsor semi-pro football teams. The Staley Company wanted to put a team together, and as part of their hiring agreement with Halas and Sternaman, it was expected that they would help form the team, and play for it as well. Both men also agreed to co-coach the team, which was known as the Decatur Staleys.

In fact, Sternaman was the first player contacted by A.E. Staley, owner of the starch company. But Sternaman was more interested in getting his degree in mechanical engineering, and went back to Illinois to do so. Staley then contacted Halas, who was more enthusiastic, and Sternaman eventually joined him in the company.

In 1921, the team was sold by the company to Halas and Sternaman, who moved the team to Chicago. They agreed to keep the name "Staley" for one season. After one season, the team became the Bears.

Sternaman played running back for the team for eight years, while also serving as co-coach. For many of the years, the quarterback of the team was Sternaman's younger brother Joey.

For several years, the Sternamans were the main source of scoring for the team. Joey also handled all kicking duties. But when Red Grange used his popularity from the 1925 barnstorming tour of the country to create a new football league called the American Football League, Joey Sternaman jumped ship and joined the Chicago Bulls of the new league.

By the late 1920s, Halas and Sternaman had grown apart as partners. They had differing opinions about how the offense would run, and eventually agreed to hire Ralph Jones to coach the team so they could both get out of that position. The two owners had differing positions on the team, although they were sort of unofficial. Halas was more the face of the franchise from the public standpoint, while Sternaman used his business background to help run things on the financial end.

By 1932, however, the financial end wasn't working out. Players were costing more money, and the bottom line was creeping up and eating into extra funds. Eventually, after much negotiation between the two friends, it was decided Halas would buy out Sternaman's shares of the team for $38,000, to be paid out in installments.

There was a time limit to the deal, and if Halas did not make all the payments in time, he would have to turn over his share of the Bears to Sternaman. According to details offered by Halas over the years, he got the final payment of $5,000 to his friend with five minutes to spare.

In 2013, the Sternaman family gave to the Pro Football Hall of Fame several boxes worth of documents left over from the days Dutch Sternaman owned the team. The documents, which are on display at the Hall of Fame museum in Canton, Ohio, included player contracts, coaching paperwork, game programs, and team-related correspondence.

99 Dan Hampton

Dan Hampton was born in Oklahoma, played in Arkansas, and came to the Bears as one tough hombre.

In 1979 the Bears used a draft pick they got from Tampa Bay to select Hampton with the fourth pick in the first round. He looked like a football player. Tall (6'5") and thick, Hampton played to his size.

Hampton did not start playing football until his junior year in high school, when the coach saw him in the marching band and decided he would be well suited to play. It took him little time to draw the attention of Division I schools, including Arkansas.

As a Razorback, Hampton was named the Southwest Conference Defensive Player of the Year for 1978. His senior year he had 18 tackles behind the line of scrimmage. When he got to the Bears, he was an immediate impact player, as defensive coordinator Buddy Ryan liked what he saw. Hampton contributed at both defensive tackle and defensive end, a luxury Ryan utilized with formation changes. Like players from a bygone era, Hampton received All-NFL honors at both defensive end and defensive tackle over his career.

Hampton received the nickname "Danimal" for his style of play on the field, but he was an engaging member of an engaging team off of it. With his southern drawl and way of living, he was a breath of fresh air in Chicago, which appreciated the fact that Hampton never seemed to take a play off.

By 1983, Hampton had the first of 12 major knee surgeries, but he was still starting in 1985 when the Bears had the greatest defense of all time. Hampton played on through all of his injuries and last played for the Bears in 1990, allowing his career to touch three separate decades.

In 1983, Hampton received recognition by signing a new contract with the Bears. Actually, he signed three new contracts, one for each year, and the total amount of the deal was approximately $1 million, making him the highest-paid defensive lineman in the league despite being in the league all of three years.

In 1985, Hampton made a permanent move to defensive end in order to allow rookie William "the Refrigerator" Perry to move into the starting lineup at defensive tackle. By the end of his career, Hampton had been selected to the Pro Bowl twice as a defensive tackle and twice as a defensive end.

Along with defensive lineman Steve McMichael, Hampton decided not to participate in the Bears' rallying-cry video and recording "The Super Bowl Shuffle." The Shuffle was recorded prior to the end of the season (the day after the team's only loss that season, in fact), and Hampton found it inappropriate to celebrate the team's success before it had even had success.

Hampton also did not attend the White House ceremony in 2011 celebrating the 25th anniversary of the Super Bowl team. That team did not get to go to the White House in 1986 because the Space Shuttle Challenger exploded two days before their intended date with then President Ronald Reagan. When Barack Obama became president, he decided to invite the team to an anniversary celebration, but Hampton did not attend due to his dislike of Obama.

He also said it was "time to let it go" in reference to the continued adulation of the Super Bowl–champion team.

Hampton played his entire career with the Bears. He finished with 57 sacks in 157 games. He was enshrined in the Pro Football Hall of Fame in 2002.

100 Punters

So, who were the best punters in Chicago Bears history?

Who cares?

Just kidding! It's wrong to think punters do not have an effect on the success of a team, even if it is very hard to quantify just how they manage to do so.

Unfortunately, punting sometimes feels like giving up. Teams punt because they don't think they can get the first down on fourth down. They punt to get the ball out of their end. They punt and hope the defense can provide a turnover that will put the offense in a better position.

In the old days of football, just about anyone would be called on to punt. With as many as four players in the backfield at one time, a punt could be a good surprise move.

But in the last three decades of the 20th century and the first decade of the 21st, the Bears were lucky to have several good punters for several good years.

In terms of longevity, the leader in the clubhouse was Bob Parsons, who played for the Bears from 1972 to 1983 in 170 games.

Parsons was good enough as a punter out of Penn State that the Bears selected him in the fifth round of the 1972 draft. He also played tight end, and caught 19 passes in his 12 years with the Bears. He also served as the Bears' third quarterback during his time with the team.

As a punter, Parsons averaged 38.7 yards per punt out of 884 kicks. He had three seasons in which he averaged over 40 yards per punt.

In 1984, after Dave Finzer couldn't hold on to it, the punting job went to Maury Buford. Buford was drafted out of Texas Tech

The Year 2019

If you are reading this before the year 2019, prepare yourself for a major event, because that is when the Bears will celebrate their 100th year of existence and it should be a momentous occasion.

If you are reading this after 2019...how was it?

by the San Diego Chargers in 1982, but came to the Bears in 1985 and was a member of the Super Bowl XX championship team. If you want to get a look at him, check out "The Super Bowl Shuffle" and keep an eye on the "Shufflin' Crew" backup band. Buford is playing cowbell.

Buford had 137 punts in two seasons for the Bears and averaged over 41.5 yards per punt. He lost his job in 1987 but came back to punt for the Bears again in 1989 and punted for them for another three years. By the time he was done he had kicked in 80 games for the Bears.

Todd Sauerbrun, who played his college ball at West Virginia, was drafted in the second round of the 1995 NFL Draft by the Bears, one of the highest slots for a punter in NFL draft history. He had 55 punts in 1995 and punted for the Bears through the 1999 season.

Third on the list of all-time Bears punters, at least in terms of number of kicks (behind Parsons and Brad Maynard), was Bobby Joe Green, who played for the Bears from 1962 to 1973 and was a member of the great 1963 Bears championship team. Green averaged 42.6 yards per kick at a time when punting numbers weren't usually that high.

The Bears did not draft Brad Maynard. He was in the league for four years with the New York Giants before the Bears got him in 2001. But Maynard kicked for the Bears for 10 seasons, finishing with 878 kicks. But what was best about Maynard was his ability to turn punts into a new set of downs for the team. He passed the ball out of either punt or field goal formation seven times in his career with the Bears and completed five of them, two of them for touchdowns.

The list of top 10 career Bears punters includes some other less notable names, but what is funny is that the No. 9 punter in both yards and attempts is the same guy—Hall of Fame quarterback Sid Luckman.

Acknowledgments

Several years ago, when Triumph Books asked me to write *100 Things Bulls Fans Should Know & Do Before They Die,* it was a fairly easy assignment. After all, I had lived the entire history of the Bulls. I moved into the Chicago area as a grade schooler the year the Bulls got their start in 1966. Eventually, I became a sportswriter and traveled with the Bulls for more than a decade. I covered them three different times for three different media outlets. I knew the fun facts, all I had to do was dig up the details.

Although my children believe I am old enough to have been around for the start of the Bears, that is not true. My parents weren't even born when the Bears came into existence in 1919. My relationship with the Bears began in 1966 as a child, and my professional relationship began in 1985 when I covered the team for United Press International. Good season to cover the team, don't you think?

I covered the Bears until 1988 for UPI before joining the *Daily Herald* to cover the Bulls. In 1999, I switched beats and became the backup beat writer for the Bears until 2007. I got to cover the 2006 Super Bowl team, and got to attend a free Jimmy Buffett concert that weekend in Miami. So I have a connection with the team, but only in the most recent half of its existence.

Researching the team from 1919 proved to be a challenge. There was a lot of information to digest, and some of it was sketchy. Then again, some of the topics from the beginning days of the team, most notably the life story of George Halas, proved to be so extensive, I didn't know where to stop with it.

It's important for today's Bears fans to understand what came before the 1985 Super Bowl championship. I hope this book paints a bit of that picture.

I am a newspaper man, and a big fan of libraries. As such, I found a great deal of the information for this book from newspaper archives or books found at the Park Ridge Public Library. But I am also a modern-day researcher, and the Internet provided much of the information as well. A challenge occasionally came when source material argued over particulars, but that just provided me more opportunity to research further, which was fun work.

The books and websites I used are listed in the bibliography. But I want to extend my appreciation for those people with whom I worked in my stints covering the Bears.

So, thanks to my *Daily Herald* colleagues Bob LeGere (loved the concourse walks), Mike Imrem, Barry Rozner, and John Dietz. Thanks to my United Press International colleague and mentor Randy Minkoff.

I would like to say "thanks for putting up with me" to my friendly competitors from the *Chicago Tribune, Chicago Sun-Times,* and *Daily Southtown,* namely Melissa Isaacson, John Mullin, Dan Pompei, Mike Mulligan, Mark Potash, Brad Biggs, Kelly Quain, and Phil Arvia.

If I forget anybody, it's because I'm old. But not that old.

Thank you to my wife, Janice, and my kids, Haley, Dan, Lindsey, and Kyle, for the support and love they have provided me.

—Kent McDill

Sources

Books

Bears in Their Own Words, by Richard Whittingham, Contemporary Books, Chicago, IL, 1991

Amazing Tales from the Chicago Bears' Sidelines, by Steve McMichael, Phil Arvia and John Mullin, Sports Publishing, New York, NY 2011

The Chicago Bears: From George Halas to Super Bowl XX: An Illustrated History, by Richard Whittingham, Simon & Schuster, New York, NY, 1979, 1982, 1986

The Rise and Self-Destruction of the Greatest Football Team in History, by John Mullin, Triumph Books, Chicago, IL, 2005

Soldier Field, a Stadium and Its City, by Liam T. A. Ford, University of Chicago Press, 2009

Fifty Greatest Plays in Chicago Bears History, by Lew Freedman, Triumph Books, Chicago, IL, 2008

Websites

www.grantland.com
www.ehow.com
www.profootballhof.com
www.chicaogbears.com
www.bearshistory.com
www.espnchicago.com
www.nfl.com
www.espn.com
www.bleacherreport.com
www.packers.com
www.fantasyfootballchallenge.com

Newspapers

Chicago Tribune
Chicago Sun-Times
Daily Herald
Dallas Morning News
Decatur Herald-Review
Green Bay News-Chronicle
Green Bay Press-Gazette
Milwaukee Journal Sentinel